# When Teens Abuse Their Parents

# When Teens Abuse Their Parents

Barbara Cottrell

Fernwood Publishing • Halifax, Nova Scotia

Editing: Brenda Conroy
Cover image: David Armstrong
Printed and bound in Canada by: Hignell Printing Limited


A publication of:
Fernwood Publishing
Site 2A, Box 5, 32 Oceanvista Lane
Black Point, Nova Scotia, B0J 1B0
and 324 Clare Avenue
Winnipeg, Manitoba, R3L 1S3
www.fernwoodbooks.ca

Fernwood Publishing Company Limited gratefully acknowledges
the financial support of the Department of Canadian Heritage,
the Nova Scotia Department of Tourism and Culture
and the Canada Council for the Arts for our publishing program.

Library and Archives Canada Cataloguing in Publication

Cottrell, Barbara, 1945-
When teens abuse their parents / Barbara Cottrell.

ISBN 1-55266-143-1

1. Abused parents. 2. Family violence. 3. Aggressiveness (Psychology) in
children. I. Title.

HV6626.C68 2004      362.82'92      C2004-903469-3

# Contents

Acknowledgements ........................................................................ ix

Introduction .................................................................................. 1

1.  Parents' Stories ................................................................... 5
    Irene ................................................................................. 5
    Connie .............................................................................. 7

2.  What Is Parent Abuse? ..................................................... 10
    Physical Abuse .............................................................. 11
    Emotional Abuse ........................................................... 11
    Financial Abuse ............................................................. 15
    Sexual Abuse ................................................................. 16
    Parricide ......................................................................... 16
    Defining Abuse .............................................................. 16
    Naming Parent Abuse .................................................... 17
    Public Information ......................................................... 19
    Were The Old Days Any Better? .................................... 23
    Conclusion ..................................................................... 24
    Note ............................................................................... 24

3.  More Parents' Stories ...................................................... 25
    Theresa ........................................................................... 25
    Donna ............................................................................. 28
    Linda .............................................................................. 30
    Lori ................................................................................. 33
    Pauline ........................................................................... 35
    Deborah .......................................................................... 36

4.  Who Is Abused? ................................................................ 39
    Income, Ethnicity and Age ............................................. 40
    "Permissive Parents" ...................................................... 41

Mother Abuse ..................................................... 45
Parental Conflict ................................................ 52
Siblings, Relatives and Pets ................................. 55
The Common Despair .......................................... 57
Conclusion ....................................................... 61

5.  Teens Speak ........................................................ 63
Jordan ............................................................. 63
Karena ............................................................ 65
Crystal ............................................................ 68
Conclusion ....................................................... 69

6.  Who Is Doing the Abusing? ................................... 72
Gender ............................................................ 72
Age and Size ..................................................... 73
Family Violence ................................................. 74
Learned Aggression ........................................... 75
School and Peers ............................................... 78
Substance Use and Abuse ................................... 82
Mental Disabilities ............................................ 83
Guilt and Remorse ............................................. 83
Conclusion ....................................................... 84

7.  The Final Blow .................................................... 86
Clare ............................................................... 86
Mary ............................................................... 87

8.  Looking for Causes .............................................. 88
Today's World ................................................... 89
Family Stress .................................................... 91
The Stress of Poverty ......................................... 93
Parenting in Today's World .................................. 95
The School's Response ........................................ 98
Mental Illness .................................................. 99
Conclusion ...................................................... 101

9.  Information and Supports ..................................... 103
Breaking the Silence .......................................... 104
The Helping Professionals ................................... 106
Mental Health Professionals ................................ 107
Criminal Justice Professionals .............................. 109

Child Welfare Workers ....................................................... 113
The "Hot Potato" Routine................................................. 115
Success! ........................................................................... 117
Conclusion ....................................................................... 117

10. Supportive Listeners................................................... 118
Parent Support Groups .................................................. 119
Mediation, Restorative Justice and Circle Healing ............. 119
Professional Responsibility ............................................ 120
Counselling ..................................................................... 120
Social Learning Theory and Stress Theory ........................ 124
Directive and Non-directive Counselling ......................... 126
Collaborative Relationships ............................................ 128
Conclusion ....................................................................... 130
Notes ............................................................................... 130

11. The Ultimate Goal:
Regaining Control and Healing the Relationship ..................... 131
Making Changes ............................................................ 131
Self-care ......................................................................... 132
Learning about Parent Abuse ......................................... 133
Talking about the Abuse ................................................. 134
Exploring Ourselves ....................................................... 135
Being Present in Teens' Lives ......................................... 135
Acting, Not Reacting ...................................................... 137
Learning Respect ............................................................ 139
Non-punitive Approaches ............................................... 141
When Teens Leave the Home ......................................... 143
Conclusion ....................................................................... 145

12. Spreading the Word.................................................... 146
Distributing Parent Abuse Materials .............................. 146
Working with Schools and Community Groups ................ 148
Organizing Workshops .................................................... 148
Forming a Support Group ............................................... 156
Note ............................................................................... 156

Conclusion: Help Wanted .............................................. 157

Appendix One .................................................................. 160
Websites .......................................................................... 160

Appendix Two .......................................................... 164
    Workshop Handouts and Poster ........................ 164
    Parent Abuse Workshop .................................... 164
    Goals .................................................................. 164
    Workshop Poster ................................................ 164
    Workshop Outline ............................................. 166
    Workshop Questions to Stimulate Discussion .... 167
    Evaluation Sheet ............................................... 168

Afterword ............................................................... 169

References ............................................................. 170

Index ..................................................................... 175

# Acknowledgements

This book would not have been possible without the support of many people. My first thanks go to the brave parents and teens who told me their stories.

I have worked with wonderful colleagues and would like to thank Diane Kays, who had the perception to recognize parent abuse as an issue and was an invaluable resource and support throughout the research. Diane and other members of the Committee Against Woman Abuse dedicated many hours to guiding the research and distributing the materials we produced. My thanks go to committee members Catherine Hennigar-Shuh, New Start Domestic Abuse Program; Jennifer Lake, Single Parent Centre; Linda Roberts, Captain William Spry Centre; Rhea McGarva, Dalhousie Legal Aid Society; Denise Moore, Nova Scotia Advisory Council on the Status of Women; and Margie Macdonald, Sheila Drysdale and Terri Rodrigues, individual members.

Morah MacEachern, Director of the Family Services Association of Halifax; Dr. Madine Vanderplaat, St. Mary's University; Nancy Gray, Director of New Start Domestic Abuse Program, and my two exceptional research assistants, Maryanne Finlayson and Annemarie van Vuren made invaluable contributions to this work. Thanks also to the many other service providers who spoke with me about their work with parents and the teens who are abusing them, and to Sheila Lane at the J.L. Ilsley Teen Health Centre, Stacey Greenough, at the Children's Aid Society of Halifax, and Carmen Celina Moncayo, Metropolitan Immigrant Settlement Association, for helping locate parents and teens who were willing to talk to me.

I have learned a great deal from my friends and colleagues, Jackie Barclay and Haim Omer, and thank them for sharing their wisdom. My deepest thanks to Eddie Gallagher, Peter Monk, and Jerry Price for endlessly discussing with me their experiences working with abused parents and their teens, and to Haja Molter, for supporting this work.

Beate Blasius, Judith Meyrick and Victor Thiessen tirelessly read and reread the chapters as they were written and provided many helpful suggestions. Anne Bishop, Belinda Burt, Catherine Browning, Jan Morrell and my sister, Sue Cottrell, also gave me invaluable feedback and encouragement.

Although the views expressed in this book may not reflect those of Health Canada and Justice Canada, I am grateful for their support of the research. The National Clearinghouse on Family Violence deserves thanks for publishing and nationally distributing my report on parent abuse. Thanks also to the helpful staff at Fernwood Publishing, in particular, Errol Sharpe for encouraging me to write this book, Brenda Conroy for editing and Beverley Rach for the design.

# Introduction

This book is called *When Teens Abuse Their Parents* because that best describes the topic, but, as with most books, numerous titles were considered. Parents who had experienced abuse offered suggestions. One mother thought it should be called *Disorder,* because that described the family and the social system in which she was parenting. Well-functioning families are a natural hierarchy, with parents in leadership positions. In families where teens are abusing their parents, the teens are in control and disorder reigns. Disorder also describes the system of supports available to parents who try to get help to regain leadership in their families. Another suggestion was *Help Wanted*, which describes one mother's isolation and frustration.

In a British social work magazine writer Yasmin Alibhai-Brown states:

> I do believe that increasing numbers of ordinary children ... are rougher, more inconsiderate, abusive and occasionally violent today than in previous decades.... It could happen to any one of us ... and when it does you quickly understand how grotesquely unfair it is to be held solely responsible for the abuse you are suffering from the child you brought into the world. It must make parents feel utterly disconsolate and betrayed, not to mention guilty, that it is all their fault. (Alibhai-Brown 2003: 22)

I wrote this book for these parents. I hope it will also be a useful tool for the people who try to help them: friends and family, counsellors, social workers, police and probation officers and all the other people parents turn to for help. Although I do discuss fathers, and I have included stories told by teens, the topic is told from the mothers' point of view. It is a painful topic, and you may want to read it in small bites and have a friend on hand who will come over for a cup of tea and give you the chance to talk about it.

The book is based on my research on parent abuse, which began in 1995. At a meeting of a local committee against woman abuse, Diane Kays, a therapist, asked, "Does anyone have any information about the abuse of women by their teenage children?" Diane's clients were telling her stories about being yelled at and pushed around by their teens. None of us knew anything about it. We searched our libraries of family violence information and were surprised when we didn't find the topic mentioned. Wider library searches turned up a few academic papers that were based on data from the United States and were contradictory. Counsellors, social workers and other professionals told us they were hearing more and more anecdotal evidence of this form of family violence among their clients but had no written information. The committee wanted to find out if this was indeed an emerging issue, and we organized a one-day conference, The Abuse of Women By Their Teenage Children, in May 1995. Overwhelmingly, both professionals and parents reported that this was a critical problem but little was known about it or why it was happening. We didn't know what form it took, if mothers or fathers were more likely to be the victim or if boys or girls were more likely to be abusive. Parents said they often did not know what behaviours they should tolerate from their children, how to handle the violence or where to seek help. Professionals, including clinical therapists, family counsellors, police, teachers and recreation workers, were unsure how far they should intervene and what their role should be.

At the conference, there was overwhelming support for the committee to try to find out the nature and extent of the problem and to develop much needed resource materials. We began to think about what people needed to know. We concluded that there were seven key questions:

- What is parent abuse?
- How widespread is parent abuse?
- Who is the abuser?
- Who is being abused?
- How is the family affected?
- Why is the abuse happening?
- Where can families get help? (Cottrell 2001: 1)

These questions became the basis for research funded by Health

Canada and sponsored by the Captain William Spry Community Centre, the Committee Against Woman Abuse and the Family Service Association of the Halifax Regional Municipality. My colleague, MaryAnne Finlayson, and I met with parents, professionals and adolescents in group discussions and in formal and informal individual interviews. We listened to forty-five parents who had experienced parent abuse; to thirty-four community workers, clinicians, academics and other professionals; and to thirty-nine teenagers. A number of people interviewed self-identified as both a professional and a parent of an abusive teen.

A pamphlet, an eight-page summary and a final report documented the research findings. At the request of Health Canada, further interviews were conducted in 1999 to update the material, and *Parent Abuse: The Abuse of Parents by Their Teenage Children* was published by Health Canada (Cottrell 2001). This publication is available free of charge from the National Clearinghouse on Family Violence (1-800-267-1291 <www.hc-sc.gc.ca/nc-cn>. Further details of the research can be found in an article I wrote with social worker Peter Monk (Cottrell 2004).

The committee received funding from Justice Canada in 2000 to collect stories from parents who had been abused. Annemarie van Vuren worked with me on this project. A number of the stories are included in this book, in the words of the parents and teens or as summaries of their stories. In 2004, I worked with Dr. Madine VanderPlaat, a sociologist at St. Mary's University in Halifax, to conduct the research on parent abuse in immigrant families, also funded by Justice Canada.

For this book I have drawn on information I collected during these research projects. All names of parents and their teens have been changed to protect their privacy. I also relied heavily on the work of four practising counsellors who work with abused parents and their teens: Haim Omer, a psychologist in Israel, who wrote *Parental Presence: Reclaiming a Leadership Role in Bringing Up Our Children*; Peter Monk, a social worker in British Columbia, who wrote *Adolescent-To-Parent Violence: A Qualitative Analysis of Emerging Themes*, his masters' thesis; Jerome Price, Director of the Michigan Family Institute and author of *Power and Compassion: Working with Difficult Adolescents and Abused Parents*; and Eddie Gallagher, an Australian social worker.

The book is about the what, who, how and why of parent abuse. Two parents' stories are given in Chapter One. Chapter Two attempts to define parent abuse and Chapter Three offers more parents' stories. Chapter Four answers the question, Who is abused? Chapter Five gives stories from the teens' point of view, and Chapter Six looks at the teens who are doing the abusing. Two mothers describe key incidents in their lives with their teens in Chapter Seven. The complexity of causes, and the social, familial and individual roots of parent abuse, including the stress families experience, the problems with school and the role of mental illness are discussed in Chapter Eight. Above all things, the difficulty parents have in finding adequate information and supports is the underlying theme of this book, and this is discussed in Chapter Nine. Chapter Ten offers guidelines to parents about finding support and suggestions for things service providers may want to consider, and Chapter Eleven is about parents' ultimate goal: regaining control and healing the relationship with their teen. Chapter Twelve offers suggestions for what communities can do to address the issue.

# 1. Parents' Stories

In order to find out about parent abuse, we began by asking parents to tell us their stories. Speaking about their families was difficult and upsetting for them, but they did find some measure of relief in the process. It took courage for them to speak the unspeakable, and I am extremely grateful to them. A number of stories are included in the book. We begin with Irene and Connie.

## Irene

Irene is a single parent. Problems with her son, Colin, started when he was fourteen. He was diagnosed with Attention Deficit Hyperactivity Disorder and placed on Ritalin, but, encouraged by his father, often refused to take his medication. Colin began using marijuana, hitting and punching his mother, breaking up the house, destroying the siding and punching holes in the walls. He tore the telephone off the wall and broke the lock on Irene's bedroom door. He refused to obey the rules, intimidated Irene by pushing up against her in a threatening manner and tried to provoke her into hitting him. He told his mother she was crazy, that he had friends and she did not, and that this was proof there was something wrong with her. He instructed his friends to ignore her.

Tired, depressed and anxious, living with an abusive son in a rundown house, Irene finally pulled together the energy to seek help. She talked to a neighbour who also had problems with her son and called the school for help. The principal was very supportive, but the school was not equipped to handle Colin's learning and behaviour problems, and Colin refused to accept discipline at school or do his homework. Irene talked to counsellors, the alternative justice agency and child protection. Irene felt they blamed her for Colin's behaviour and saw his father as an ally. He said he did not find Colin difficult to live with, but he usually left Colin on his own with money in his pocket and no supervision. Irene felt the professionals were misjudging the situation and believed that the social worker breached confidentiality when she discussed the case with another counsellor. Irene also thought that Colin was working the system and manipulating the social worker. When the social worker left, Colin would threaten Irene. She wanted the social worker to find a foster or group home for her son, but none was available.

Eventually, in spite of feeling like a failure, she had no choice but to call the police and file charges of assault and damaging property against Colin. But the first charges disappeared. Irene says she was so new at the game, she probably did something wrong. Colin's father told him to retaliate and have his mother charged. Irene believes Colin's abusive behaviour towards her was worse after he'd had contact with his father.

For about a month, Colin's behaviour improved. He hugged his mother and talked to her. Then the abuse started again. Irene said she felt like she was dying. She had stomach and head pain, and when blood work showed no physical cause, the doctor prescribed sleeping pills, but they made her sluggish in the daytime and she had to stop taking them.

When Colin threatened to kill her, Irene again called the police. At first she felt very sad but realized that it was up to Colin to make a difference. In court, Colin admitted to the assault and that he had trouble with his temper. Irene told the judge that Colin's father would not support her and made the situation worse by accusing her of causing Colin's problems and making him angry.

Colin went to live with an aunt, but Irene was lonely without him, and she welcomed him when he wanted to come home again. She made it clear to her son that if he did not stick to his end of the bargain — to refrain from abusing her and from using drugs — she would call the police and he would be charged.

Soon after Colin's return home, the abuse began again. This time, Irene told him she had found out that she has the right to defend herself and could not be charged for hitting him in self defence. She told him she didn't think he was a bad person, but he was no longer allowed to abuse her. Colin broke down and cried. This was a huge breakthrough in his own understanding of the abuse.

Irene believes she did the right thing because everything worked out well in the end. Her experiences helped her to overcome her shyness and become a person who speaks out. She speaks to other parents who have difficult children and feels that finally she is no longer isolated.

## Connie

Connie and her husband have two daughters, Joanne, who is twenty-four, and Emily, twenty-one. When the children were little, Connie felt they had a very good family life together. Like any family, they had a few problems but were always able to work them out. Joanne worked hard at school, kept her curfew and talked to her parents about what was happening in her life. She had her moments, but never showed any disrespect to her parents. They could count on her. Emily was different. She was a difficult, colicky infant and at school she was smart but never opened a book. She wouldn't obey her curfew and would try to take advantage of her parents. Even as young as five years old, the rules were for everybody else, not her.

When she was in grade nine she started smoking cigarettes, although her parents did not allow it in their home. Later, when she borrowed the car, she wouldn't have it home when she was supposed to, and Connie's husband would have to go out looking for her. As she got into grades eleven and twelve, she would answer back, and Connie never knew what was coming next. She did well at school and went on to university, but she couldn't get into the program she wanted and blew her first year partying. Her parents told her that when she could show that she was mature and responsible they would cover half her costs for her second year. She was drinking alcohol and using marijuana, and her behaviour became harder to handle. Her parents never knew if she was going to holler, curse and throw things at them or be smiley and nice. Connie began to realize that Emily was sweet when she wanted something, but if she didn't get her own way she'd call her mother a bitch, curse and throw things at her. One time, when Connie needed the telephone and asked Emily to get off, Emily hit her mother. Connie said, "She hit me hard and it broke my heart. It was such a shock. I felt like hitting her back. It was hard not to, but I didn't, thank goodness. I just had a terrible feeling."

On a trip from the hospital, Connie said that as Emily had driven in, Connie was going to drive home. Emily grabbed the keys, kicked her mother, and jumped in the van and took off. Connie was crying so hard, she couldn't talk, and a passer-by called 911. That was probably the last thing in the world Connie wanted, but she wasn't thinking straight. The police came and Connie had to tell them the story. She felt torn, telling the police about her own daughter. One of the police officers told Connie he knew it was terrible but that it happens all the time and shared with her that his stepson attacks him. That made Connie feel better.

Connie decided not to lay charges against Emily because that could affect her whole life. Connie's husband wanted charges laid. It was a difficult choice, because they knew the abuse could get worse. The officer gave Connie his card and said if anything ever happened again, she should call him.

Emily's behaviour affected the whole family. Joanne tried very hard at first to help her sister but she soon got fed up. She thought Connie was crazy to put up with it. Joanne's reproach really hurt, although Connie knew she was right. She said, "I'd tell her, 'You'll be a mother someday maybe and you'll understand,' but nobody, nobody, can understand."

Emily's behaviour took its toll on her father. Nothing was within reason, Emily was not dependable, and he didn't know how to handle it. She never hit her father though.

No one outside the family ever saw what was going on because, except for the day at the hospital, Emily never abused her parents in public. Connie was isolated and felt she had nowhere to turn. She says doesn't know how she survived it. She was very depressed and couldn't really sleep or eat, and took a mild sleeping drug because, as she put it, "I wasn't in good shape for myself or anybody else." At first Connie was too embarrassed to look for help or talk to anyone about what was happening, but after a while she talked to her brother, who had trouble with his own son and was very understanding.

Connie and her husband tried to get professional help. They consulted a number of doctors, and Emily went to a psychiatrist once. Connie told the psychiatrist she thought Emily's behaviour was unacceptable, but he said Emily was young and didn't seem concerned. Emily refused to go back to the psychiatrist, and, as Connie said, "If she didn't want to help herself, how could anybody else help her?"

Connie happened to see an article in the paper about a workshop for abused parents, and she suddenly recognized that it described her. The workshop helped her see that she wasn't alone, that parent abuse is, in fact, quite common. Connie has tried to think about what would make things different. She feels that parents have to learn and stumble on the way, and they don't want to speak up because they feel embarrassed and figure it's their fault, that they're bad parents. Connie knows she made mistakes and questioned herself till she felt crazy. She knows there is no cut-and-dried recipe for parenting: parents can successfully do one thing with one child, but the same approach with another child could be a disaster. Looking back, she wonders if they were not strict enough with Emily. Perhaps they didn't enforce the rules enough. But, she says, sometimes your guard gets down and you just get tired and frustrated, because teens always nag at you and just never give up. Sometimes it's easier to say yes than no. And that's the problem. Eventually, Connie and her husband knew that they could not keep putting up with the abuse and decided to lay charges if it ever happened again.

It's been a year since they made their decision clear. Emily is no longer living with her parents, and she has a good job. Connie thinks that Emily realizes what she put her family through and is trying to make amends. Connie feels "quite good about how things are now." She thinks Emily will be alright but wouldn't wish anybody else to have to go through what she did: "You do so much for your children and you never expect to be treated like that. It seems that they lash out at the people who do the most for them, so mothers really bear the brunt of it. You try so hard, but that isn't real life."

# 2. What Is Parent Abuse?

*He kicked me in the face and threatened to slit our throats. The most damaging, though, was the verbal abuse.*

Parents' accounts of the abuse they have suffered can be graphic and frightening. Parents have been hit, punched, slapped, kicked and thrown down stairs by their teenage children. They have been shoved, spat at, shut in closets and emotionally abused, often with threats and constant put-downs. While the emotional and less severe physical forms of abuse are more difficult to recognize, they are the most common and are no less painful. Jerome Price, Director of the Michigan Family Institute and author of an excellent book for therapists who work with abused parents, designed a levels of aggression chart to help parents and counsellors identify the seriousness of the child's behaviour:

> The Six Levels of Aggression
> Level 1:   Petulant child
> Level 2:   A flair for the dramatic
> Level 3:   The beginnings of damage
> Level 4:   Threatening gestures and damaging possessions
> Level 5:   People get hurt, usually accidentally (e.g., when the teen throws things)
> Level 6:   Serious danger and physical harm.
> (Price and Cottrell 2002)

This chapter describes the ways teens abuse their parents and discusses the parents' and service providers' difficulty in naming these behaviours as abusive. It also explores whether parent abuse is a new phenomenon or if it is just a secret that has been well kept for a long time.

## Physical Abuse

The most visual form of abuse is physical abuse. Parents who are physically abused are usually also emotionally abused. Sarah and Ron, a warm, friendly couple in their forties, were victims of severe physical and emotional abuse by their son, Jason. When Jason was sixteen years old, six feet tall and 250 pounds, he hit his mother in the head with a bottle, kicked her in the face and shoved, pushed and slapped her. He held a knife to his parents and threatened to slit their throats. He told them he had a gun and was going to kill them and often said he should have done it while he had the chance. He would block the door so Sarah couldn't get out and once pulled the phone from the wall so she couldn't call the police. He punched holes in walls, cut up wooden chairs with a knife, burned his mattress and kicked in his bedroom door. He argued and ran his parents down, called them nasty names and repeatedly said he hated them. He told them what to do and when to do it, stole from them and sold the clothes they bought him. Once he ran away but called home continuously, threatening to steal a car and break into a store. He repeatedly threatened to hurt himself or commit suicide.

## Emotional Abuse

Irene's story from Chapter One shows that her son was physically abusive, but he was also very threatening. Like many mothers, Irene was filled with fear when her son stood too close and "in her face." The teen's tone, rather than the actual words or behaviour, was offensive and hurtful. Holly told me this story: One day her fifteen-year-old daughter, Jane, walked into Holly's bedroom. A set of bongo drums was on the floor, and Jane nonchalantly tapped them with her foot. "What're these?" she asked in a slightly bored tone. Holly explained that they were very special. They had belonged to her grandfather for many years, and he was giving them to Holly's friend, who had just started drumming. "In fact," Holly said, "if you pass them up to me, I'll run over and give them to her now." With an almost imperceptible sneer as a response, Jane turned and walked out of the room. Holly told me that as she bent down to pick up the drums, she felt little, dismissed, worthless. "I feel so put down I could scream. Sometimes I just want to leave this family and live on my own. I'm a professional with college degrees and a responsible job, and yet there are times when she treats me as though I'm so stupid I wouldn't know how to make chocolate chip cookies. Is that parent abuse?" Holly asked. This chapter will explore the answer to that question.

My research with parents leads me to believe that most parent abuse is manipulation and that teens use a wide spectrum of physical, emotional and/or financial behaviours in an attempt to get their own way. Whether the abuse is physical or emotional, it is bullying and meant to demean, instil fear in and undermine parents, to make the victims feel bad about themselves by attacking their self-confidence. Physical abuse hurts the soul as much as the body. One mother said her daughter would walk past and give her a smack or a push, just to let her know who was in control. It didn't really hurt the mother physically, but it reduced her to a wreck. At a workshop for parents, Mary talked of the physical abuse she and her husband had suffered, and then said:

> *The most damaging, though, was the verbal abuse. Our daughter was very quick to tell us how lousy we were as individuals and as parents. That is unbelievably hard to hear on a regular basis, and it certainly affected our feelings about ourselves.*

Parents are constantly told they are stupid and can't do anything right. They are called names and told they are idiots or weirdos. Yelling and arguing are common. Teens challenge with, "I don't have to do anything you say!" or they are sarcastic, critical and belittling, laughing in the parent's face and swearing at them. "You bitch!" and "I hate you!" are taunts that are intended to hurt. One mother said:

> *She tells me I'm a worthless piece of trash and that if she knew she'd get away with it she'd throw me down the stairs and kill me. She calls me a f—ing bitch, both in front of her friends and when she's alone. Every day it gets worse. She says I'm useless, a coward, no wonder her dad left me. But she knows that I left him!*

Being frightened by a teen can be as severe as actually being hit. As Connie said, "When you see somebody fly into a rage like that, it's very scary. Very, very scary." One teen threatened that a friend would break her mother's knees if her mother didn't do what the teen wanted. While this mother didn't really believe her daughter, it left her insecure and anxious because she was never sure. Teens who threaten to kick in the walls if their mothers don't do what they are told or to rip the phone out of the wall if they don't hang up immediately can be very frightening. Breaking things, punching holes in the walls and throwing objects are common forms of threatening behaviour. Underlying those actions is the often unspoken: "and your head will be next." It leaves the parent with the unmistakable message, "If I can do this to a wall, I can do it to you. I'm in control here."

Destroying the parent's property can be a form of abuse. Emily forgot her keys one day and rather than wait for her mother to return home, she smashed in the door. Other mothers told us that their teens damaged their houses when the mothers hid to avoid being hit: "She's punched me in the mouth and thrown things at me. When she came after me, I hid in the bathroom, and she kicked a hole in the bathroom door." Another mother described how her child broke phones by slamming them against walls, broke dishes and personal things and threw away her mother's belongings before she "generally trashed my apartment." Living in a house their teen has trashed increases a parent's distress. Many do as their teens say because they can't afford to fix broken walls and doors and don't have the skills to do it themselves. One mother told me she would drive her son to town on demand because he threatened to kick in the walls if she didn't. Another said she gets off the phone when told so that her son doesn't pull it out of the wall.

Teens also control their parents by threatening to kill or harm themselves. Jerome Price says that teens often fantasize about how sorry everyone will be when they are gone and imagine the scene around their graves. He tells of one teen who told her mother: "If you don't do what I want I'll go and sleep with drug dealers" (Price and Cottrell 2002). He calls this the Four in One Threat because in one short sentence the teen has threatened to run away, expose herself to a sexually transmitted disease like AIDS, run the risk of getting pregnant and live a life of drugs and crime. Self-harm can take many forms and include such things as eating disorders and refusing to take care of themselves. Haim Omer tells of a boy who was very ill and had to take regular medication. The boy used the threat of not taking his medication as a way of controlling his father. He would "forget" to take his pills or leave them somewhere. The more his father pleaded, the more irresponsible the son would behave. Eventually, the child had his father in a state of terror about his son's health (Omer 2000: 127–132).

Playing "mind games," intentionally telling lies and keeping secrets to upset their parents or make them doubt their sanity also constitute emotional abuse. This seventeen-year-old teen was fully aware of the impact of his nasty behaviour:

*I used to play mind games with my parents, but I never hit them. I'd do little things to upset them, to get them going. Like I'd take the batteries out of the TV and VCR remote controls and hide them, then watch my father go nuts trying to change the channel. Or, I'd lock up a little box in my room and put it under the bed, but leave a corner sticking out, like I'd meant to hide it. There'd be nothing in it, but it would drive my parents crazy thinking I had dope or something in my room.*

An act that could be a harmless, even funny, practical joke can be devastating when the intention is malicious.

The threat of loss is also used to control parents. Maria was a grandmother who was very close to her daughter's baby. When her daughter wanted to inflict emotional pain on Maria, she would lock herself in her room and refuse to let her mother see the baby. When the baby was crying and in distress, Maria felt even more helpless and thought she had no choice but to give in to her daughter's demands.

Women talk of their teens trying to drive them insane, of being told they are "crazy" and beginning to feel that way. One mother said when she asked her daughter to wash the dishes, her daughter would wash her own but not her mother's. This teen would turn up the thermostat and leave her window open even though she knew that heating was expensive. By these actions she let her mother know who was in control, and she told her mother, "I'm sticking around here to drive you crazy." Another mother said her daughter stole cigarettes and money and had her mother second-guessing herself, "Did I put that money there or not? She had me convinced I was crazy." As we saw in Connie's story, even pleasantness and remorse can be manipulative. Connie's daughter, Emily, had pleasant moments, but Connie and her husband soon realized Emily was "nice" only when she wanted something.

Emotional abuse includes:
• intimidating the parent
• maliciously playing mind games
• trying to make parent think they are crazy
• making unrealistic demands on the parent, such as insisting they drop what they're doing to comply with the child's orders
• purposely not telling the parent where they're going or what they're doing
• running away from home or staying out all night
• lying
• threatening to hurt, damage or kill the parent or someone else
• making manipulative threats, such as threatening to run away, commit

suicide or otherwise hurt themselves without really intending to do
so
• degrading the parent or other family members
• withholding affection and avoiding, shunning or ignoring
• controlling the running of the household.

## Financial Abuse

Financial abuse such as stealing, borrowing without permission, demanding money and misusing their parent's belongings is common.
Women carry their purses around with them all the time they are in the
house, keep the telephone under lock and key and take their cheque-
books and jewellery to work. One woman said, "Anything pawnable,
like my camera and binoculars, are gone." Another said, "I still keep my
money in my pocket, I don't use a wallet because he would steal from
me. He wiped out my entire savings because he got hold of my PIN
number." Connie's daughter, Emily, would borrow the car and not
bring it back for two or three days. Stealing from parents can be used to
hurt rather than for financial gain: "He would steal precious things, not
necessarily things that were expensive. Their importance was sentimental, for example, a gold medallion I received from my grandmother for
my first communion."

Teens also financially abuse by attempting to force their parents to
spend more money than they can afford. Parents face tremendous
ongoing pressure from the culturally pervasive idea that they should
provide their children with material possessions, and abusive teens
capitalize on this. They feed into their parents' feelings of obligation and
inadequacy. Most teens try to convince their parents to provide them
with the latest in brand-name goods, but will listen to reason and take no
for an answer. Abusive teens won't:

> You can't reason with her. If she wants something that I can't afford, I
> explain it to her and she says "I don't want to hear this." She thinks
> everything's my fault. I even took out a bank loan because she wanted a
> whole new bedroom suite, but it's never enough, she always wants more.

Financial abuse includes:
• stealing money or parent's belongings (sometimes referred to as
  "borrowing" without permission)
• selling possessions, their own or the parent's
• destroying the home or parent's belongings

- demanding the parent buys things they don't feel they can afford
- incurring debts the parent must cover, e.g., damage to or theft of other's property.

## Sexual Abuse

Sexual assault was not mentioned by any of the parents, teens or service providers that I interviewed, and I have not found any literature on this form of violence. This leads me to believe that this form of abuse occurs very rarely, but I realize that it does occur. England, for instance, has recently given a high profile to the case of a fifteen-year-old who raped his mother in July 2003.

## Parricide

The most extreme act of parent abuse is murder, and some children do kill their parents. Unlike other forms of parent abuse, this is very rare, and I do not intend to discuss the topic in any depth. Suffice it to note that children sometimes commit murder when they are unable to escape from cruelty they are experiencing (Heide 1993). These children have experienced a great deal of emotional, physical and sexual damage during their lives and are not the "monsters" they are thought to be (Kelly and Totten 2002). This is sometimes, but not always, at the hands of their parents. We should remember, though, that most children who experience such harm do not commit murder.

## Defining Abuse

A definition of parent abuse that includes all three forms of abuse, physical, psychological and financial, is: "Parent abuse is any act of a child that is intended to cause physical, psychological or financial damage in order to gain control over a parent" (Cottrell 2001: 3). This definition is debatable, however, in a number of ways. First, although it appears the case for the majority, we are not sure that all teens who abuse are trying to control. We know, for instance, that teens can be abusive to their teachers, and in the school setting, it is highly unlikely they have any chance of taking control. In those cases, are the teens trying to get control and being unrealistic about their chances, or are they merely lashing out? It has been suggested that teens are not seeking control but are expressing anger. This definition also raises the question of whether an act is parent abuse when the child does not intend it to hurt or is not trying to get control over a parent. Teens might be more irresponsible and thoughtless than intentionally abusive. For instance, parents who are attacked by their severely disabled children may be unclear whether the attack is intended to hurt. Others suggest that the teen's motive is irrelevant and the behaviour is abusive only when the parents are afraid (personal communication with Peter Monk, 2003).

Another important question is who defines parent abuse. Angela Frizzell suggests that professionals, not parents, define when a teen's behaviour is abusive rather than just "misbehaviour," and this definition does not always coincide with the family's interpretation of what is going on (1998: 32). A service provider told me that when she suggested that a client was being abused by her son, the woman told her not to talk so foolish. If the parent does not experience the behaviour as abusive, is it abuse?

Another question this definition raises is whether parent abuse should be defined as "any act," that is, a single act, or if it perhaps better to think of parent abuse as a series of acts over time. The abuse usually begins with words, but ultimately most parents, like Connie and Irene, experience more than one form of abuse. Connie would "say one word," and Emily would "flip right out," call Connie a bitch, holler and curse and throw things at her until one day, when Connie needed to use the phone and asked Emily to get off it, she hit her mother. Another parent described an incident between her son and his father that began with her son yelling at his father, "You're nothing but a f—ing cripple. I wish you'd died when you had that accident!" and accelerated to screaming and throwing. It does appear that, as with spousal abuse, if it is not stopped, the abuse gets more intense as time progresses.

## Naming Parent Abuse

Defining parent abuse may be nothing more than a word exercise, and perhaps it is not necessary to nail down a precise meaning. On the other hand, when parents have difficulty making sense of their teens' behaviour, it could be helpful for them to start by naming it as abusive. We also need to know exactly what it is we are talking about here. Whether it is physical, emotional or financial abuse, parents tolerate it for a long time before they are able to name it. Parents are not alone in this. The general public doesn't recognize or name teens' abusive behaviour either. This is, in part, because adults expect unpleasant behaviour from teens today. Helen was in the food court at a shopping mall when a teenager at the next table verbally abused his mother. After they left, she commented on the abuse to a woman sitting at the next table. The woman replied that she didn't think that was abuse, so Helen asked her what she'd call it if her husband did it to her. The woman responded, "Now that's abuse." Adults hear the word "adolescent" and think rudeness and unpleasant behaviour. Confronted with young people's rudeness, they respond with "teenagers are like that."

Teachers, community workers and other service providers, including police officers, share with parents and the general public this difficulty in recognizing and naming parent abuse. A therapist told me that, when service providers refer a family to her, she asks if the child is abusive, and the response is usually, "Not really. Just normal teenage behaviour." When she inquires what they mean by this, she is appalled to hear that they mean cursing and using foul language, yelling, slamming doors and even smashing fists on desks or walls. It is interesting that the behaviour is not named as abusive, because, no matter how "normal" it is, the behaviour is intended to hurt and control. Yelling, using foul language, being disrespectful and slamming doors are abusive.

So why is it that adults think this behaviour is normal? In part, this can be traced back to the turn of the century, when psychologist G. Stanley Hall popularized adolescence as a period of "storm and stress." Although not all teens go through obnoxious or depressed periods, many do, and the process of growing up and into adulthood can be a troubled time. Most adults admit they'd never want to be a teenager again. When babies are born they are totally dependent on their parents. As they grow, they gradually separate from their parents. They start to feed themselves and walk by themselves instead of being carried. Eventually they begin to think for themselves and parents slowly let go of the reins and give them more autonomy, allowing them to make an increasing number of their own decisions. This is called "individuating." It is rarely a smooth process. For all their bravado, when they become teenagers, children tend to be more insecure and less self-confident, and hormonal changes can make them moody, impulsive, short-sighted and self-focused. This is the time when, having had a taste of making their own decisions, teens may resist authority and be defiant at times. But there is a difference between resistance and aggression; between separating from a parent and trying to take control of a parent; between 'normal' self-absorbed teenage behaviour and parent abuse. The distinction must be made between the difficult emotions adolescents experience and their behaviour. These are two separate things. No matter how distressed or how full of angst they may be, abusive behaviour is not acceptable.

Researchers and academics, as well as parents, service providers and the general public, have also been slow to name parent abuse. Consequently, very little information exists about it. During the past few decades a considerable amount of research has been focused on various types of family violence, including spousal abuse, elder abuse and child abuse, but little of this research includes teen-to-parent violence. The first known work that identified children abusing their parents was written in 1957 (Sears), but the issue wasn't named until an American academic included a question about it on a family violence survey and published an article titled "Battered Parents: A New Syndrome" (Harbin 1979). This is a somewhat curious title because although it may not have been written about, the "syndrome," even at that time, was not "new."

Over the next twenty years, a few academic articles on parent abuse followed, but if books on family violence mention it at all, they contain merely a sentence stating that this is a problem that has been ignored. As recently as ten years ago, a Health Canada report on family violence (Dekeseredy 1993) stated that, although many young people physically victimize their parents, the problem has been practically ignored by Canadian researchers. Pamphlets and information on family violence rarely mention parent abuse. The result is that people, including parents, do not have the awareness or words to think about and describe it.

## Public Information

We don't even know how widespread parent abuse is because few Canadian statistics are available. Parentline Plus, a British non-profit organization, stated that more than a quarter of all calls they received in 2002 on their twenty-four-hour helpline were from parents concerned about aggressive behaviour from their children. A number of professionals who work with adolescents in Canada, including a child welfare supervisor, told me they believe the problem of parent abuse is as widespread as spousal abuse in our society and may have reached epidemic proportions. But official Canadian statistics to confirm this are not available. The information isn't collected. Hospitals, shelters and other institutions, such as child welfare and adolescent mental health agencies, schools and youth centres, seldom recognize, record or report the problem. Police records do not always specify the relationship between the victim and perpetrator in charges of assault, and the *Youth Criminal Justice Act* prevents access to information on charges against minors. Statistics Canada conducts regular surveys on family violence, but they do not include questions about parents who are abused by their children, so Canadian General Social Survey Reports do not include information on parent abuse. They do not even have a record of the number of children under the age of twenty-one who have killed their parents. The age of the "child" is not specified in police data, so a "child" who kills a parent could be forty years old. The dearth of information on this subject isn't confined to Canada. The following titles of academic articles on parent abuse in the United States draw attention to the lack of information on the topic: "Battered Parents in California: Ignored Victims of Domestic Violence" and "Teenage Violence Toward Parents: A Neglected Dimension of Family Violence" (Arrigo 1982; Peek et al. 1985).

The few large-scale studies that have been conducted are from the United States. They suggest that in the U.S. between 9 and 18 percent of parents are hit by their adolescent children (Agnew and Huguley 1989; Cornell and Gelles 1982; Pagelow 1989; Paulson et al. 1990; Peek et al. 1985). The hits range from "smacks" to severe physical assaults, but whatever the intensity, the proportion is somewhere between one in ten and one in five: huge by any standard. The numbers vary depending on whether the research is done by asking parents if they have ever been hit by their teen or by asking the teens if they have ever hit their parents. The numbers are also misleading because they focus on physical abuse and don't include those situations in which teens are controlling their parents by instilling fear.

It wasn't until 1996, when two community groups in Nova Scotia (the Captain William Spry Community Centre and the Family Service Association of Halifax) published an eight-page information booklet on parent abuse, that free information on the topic became available in Canada. Even this material was produced on a shoe-string budget and had a very limited distribution. Since then, Health Canada has published a report that is also available free of charge,[1] and the BC Institute Against Family Violence has prepared a fact sheet.

I have received requests for the material from people in England, Australia and the United States who tell me they have difficulty finding accessible materials in their countries. A German therapy journal recently published an article I wrote on parent abuse, because they had no information on the issue and thought their readers would be interested (Cottrell 2002). In fact, publications on the issue are so rare that people tend to confuse the term parent abuse with elder abuse, that is, the abuse of the elderly by their adult children.

So, why has the issue been ignored? Why isn't more education and information about parent abuse available? First, we have to understand how problems get attention from researchers and government. It is interesting to compare parent abuse with other forms of family violence. Twenty years ago, spousal and intimate partner abuse were seldom discussed in public. The abuse was thought to occur rarely and only among certain economic classes or cultures, the victims were blamed and little help was available. Although misinformation still abounds, Canadians now accept that intimate partner abuse occurs often and among all classes and cultures and that women do not provoke the abuse. Now, there are television programs about it, safe houses for women, specific laws and police training, and even special courts. What made the difference? Problems become issues that have to be addressed when groups of citizens get together and invite media attention. In the 1970s, the issue of woman abuse came to public attention when an English woman, Erin Pizzey, wrote a book called *Scream Quietly or The Neighbours Will Hear*. The book gained a lot of publicity, and women around the western world organized to demand services. These women were vilified, but they were extremely successful. In the main, the women who worked so hard on this issue were not victims of abuse; they were professionals who saw clients or friends and relatives suffering. It is when professionals are able to visualize services that could be put in place, that they demand them.

So why aren't professionals demanding services for victims of parent abuse? Perhaps one reason is that, in this day of cutbacks, resources to put programs in place are severely limited. An even more likely reason is that few professionals have ideas about what services are needed because parent abuse doesn't fit our preconceived notions of family violence. Family violence is usually defined as violence perpetrated by people who have power over others: parents abusing children, men abusing women. We assume that parents have power over their children and therefore are not susceptible to abuse. Families are hierarchical: parents should be in control of their children. But parent abuse is an inappropriate reversal of the socially acceptable power order in families. Clearly we don't want to go back to the old days when fathers could rule by the rod or iron fist if they so chose. Parental leadership should be loving and caring. But until service providers understand that an adolescent dominating a parent is a serious societal problem and that parent abuse must be considered a form of family violence, it will remain hidden. As long as it is hidden, parents will struggle alone to figure out what is happening in their families and how to find solutions, or worse, they will struggle with unhelpful and even damaging services.

One of the consequences of this issue being hidden is that it takes some time for parents to recognize the behaviour as abusive and actually admit it to themselves. When it first starts, parents usually understate their teenager's negative behaviour, because, for most of us, conflict between people who live together is normal. One team of researchers found that conflict between high school students and their parents occurred on average more than seven times a day (Eckstein 2002). They also found that teens had frequent conflicts with their friends and schoolmates too and concluded that conflict is an everyday part of many teenagers' lives. Conflict is not necessarily negative. It is through conflict that, as parents, we establish our position of power in our families. Parents who let children do whatever they want usually lose their leadership position in the family. Few people handle conflict well, and it is not just teens who behave badly. It is the rare person who has not ever yelled or slammed a door or pouted in an attempt to get their own way. The behaviour is abusive, but when it is occasional, most of us are prepared to live with it. It may mar our enjoyment of the day, but, if it happens rarely, we don't feel compelled to do anything about it beyond clearing the air. We have a good talk with the offender, or the one we offended, the behaviour is identified as nasty, apologies are given and accepted, and family boundaries are reset.

When the bad behaviour is ongoing, however, we have cause for concern. Abuse goes beyond sullenness and rudeness in the intent, intensity and form. Even so, it may still not be severe enough for parents to want to do anything about it, or they think they must accept it because they understand the cause. For example, they think it is a stage the child is going through, or they know that the child is mentally ill or has been a victim of abuse. Whatever the cause, abusive behaviour is an inappropriate response. We all have to make our own decision about where we draw the line. It is a personal decision, but when parents and service providers don't have sufficient information, they can find it difficult to distinguish between what is acceptable and what is not.

The silence surrounding the issue contributes to it in other ways. The lack of information limits what parents can do because they are unsure of their rights. They are unclear about what they can and cannot do to ensure their own personal safety, and about the level of authority they are allowed to exercise in the home. Teens erroneously believe they are protected from their parents' authority by law, and threaten with what Price calls "hammers ... Threats of reporting parents to child protective services for any physical restraint or aggression utilized in response to abuse behaviour" (1996: 17). This teen was misinformed but, unfortunately, her parents believed her:

> *She likes to say that we can't touch her — physically — and also seems to know that the justice system can't touch her. She'll say things like, "If I get caught they can't do anything with me. They can't prosecute you until you're sixteen."*

That teen tactic is even more powerful when parents have attempted to restrain their teens. Parents live with the threat of being charged with assault, abuse or neglect when they attempt to discipline.

The shortage of information also means that not only parents but also the general public and service providers often don't recognize what is occurring. The consequence is that parents have difficulty finding help, and the abuse continues and usually gets progressively worse.

## Were The Old Days Any Better?

Many people think teenagers weren't abusive in the past, but as social worker Peter Monk pointed out, there are old laws that suggest that parent abuse was occurring centuries ago:

> If any Childe or Children above sixteen years old and of sufficient understanding, shall Curse or smite their natural father or mother, hee or they shall be put to death; unless it can bee sufficiently testified that the parents have been unchristianly negligent … or so provoke them by extreme and cruel correction. —*1648, Law of the Puritans of Massachusetts.* (1997: 15)

> If any child or servant shall, contrary to his bounden duty, presume to assault or strike his parent or master, upon complaint or conviction thereof before two or more justices of the peace, the offender shall be whipped not exceeding ten stripes. —*1819, Illinois, Punishment of the Disobedient Child.* (16)

> A girl who assaulted her mother was taken into care "by reason of [her] vicious conduct [that] rendered her control beyond the power of the said complainant. —*1883, Pennsylvania Court judgment.* (16)

## Conclusion

The truth is we don't know how old parent abuse is, anymore than we know how widespread it is. But parent abuse is beginning to come "out of the closet" because, as a society, we are no longer prepared to tolerate any violence in the family. Researchers are now paying more attention to the issue. For instance, the December 18, 2003, issue of the Australian newspaper, *The Age,* reported that the "hidden problem of children violently attacking their mothers is to be revealed" by University of Western Sydney researchers. The investigators, who state that "the seldom-reported problem was increasing," will conduct a three-year survey of about 600 families.

Perhaps as more parents speak openly about their plight and researchers study the issue, parent abuse will get the attention it deserves and we will learn more about it. The high incidence of parent abuse will finally be acknowledged, and the responsibility for the abuse and for finding solutions will not be placed squarely on the shoulders of the parents who are bullied and abused by their teenage children. In the next chapter, I share what I discovered about these parents.

## Note

1. *Parent Abuse: The Abuse of Parents by Their Teenage Children*, a report written by Barbara Cottrell for Health Canada is available free from the National Clearinghouse on Family Violence, tel: 1-800-267-1291 or on the web: <www.hc-sc.gc.ca/nc-cn>.

# 3. More Parents' Stories

The stories of the five women included here clearly demonstrate that we cannot make any generalizations about abused parents. Three of them were physically abused, two were not. Two of the abusive teens had colic as babies, three did not. Interestingly, the two with colic showed signs of abuse early in their lives; the others didn't become abusive until they were in their teens. Four of the women had separated from partners who were abusive to them, and one had a happy, stable marriage with a supportive partner. Theresa's son was not having academic problems, the others were. The help they received from service providers varied too.

Although all kinds of parents with a wide variety of experiences is the only answer to the question of who is abused, the stories do help us to see the trials, pain and despair that all parents endure. They also vividly illustrate the hope that keeps them struggling to have loving relationships with their children.

## Theresa

Theresa's son, Michael, was a colicky baby, and even as young as two years old would pinch, bite and use his toys as weapons to get his own way. His father was very controlling and physically and emotionally abused Theresa. They divorced when Michael was three years old, and Michael's behaviour went from bad to worse. At school he and his friends were always in trouble, and Michael was constantly punished, but he seemed impervious to any form of control. The teachers thought this might be a reaction to the divorce and asked Theresa to take him to a psychologist.

When Michael was twelve, Theresa met Gary, and they married. At that time he had custody of his three children. They worked hard to build a home with boundaries and security for their combined family. For the first time Michael had siblings and a man to take Mom's affection away. He despised it.

Life for Gary became difficult when his ex-wife won custody of the girls. After much deliberation, Theresa and Gary decided to take Michael and emigrate to Canada. For almost a year they were caught up in the emotions and practicalities of moving. Then, a month before they were due to leave, they were called to the school and told that Michael had been exposed as the head of a counterfeit ring. They were mortified. It was too late for therapy before they left, and, as they thought his behaviour was perhaps a reaction to all the upset of moving, they decided to wait.

The family settled in Canada, and soon Michael learned that being bad at school got him noticed. He was transferred to a different class and his behaviour improved, but things fell apart again that summer. He started smoking weed in large amounts, and when there were no other adults around he became more "in your face," standing too close to Theresa when he spoke. It was not really what he said to her but how he said it, in short, sharp, clipped tones, telling her she was an idiot and a weirdo. Theresa and Gary knew that something was really wrong. He was climbing out of his window late at night, smoking up and stealing to support the habit. They could not leave him alone in the house. That was a bad summer.

Eventually Michael said he could not stand the family rules any longer and asked to return to his father. This was arranged and he went off without as much as a backward wave. It was difficult keeping in touch with him, because after a month or two he had been expelled, was growing dope in his father's yard and selling it, and the police were involved. He had been beaten up by his father a couple of times and had been kicked out of the house. A relative put him on a plane back to Canada, and Theresa thought he might have learned a lesson.

Michael returned to high school. His marks were quite good but his attitude was not. He was caught with a firearm and charged. At home he broke up his room, punched holes in the walls, kicked in doors and shouted strings of abuse to no one in particular. One weekend they went away and left Michael with friends, but he got back into the house and had a drugs, drink and sex party for the neighbourhood. Whenever Theresa spoke to him, his stock reply was an angry "whatever."

Gary had a new job and again the family moved. At the same time, Gary's eldest daughter, Deborah, joined them in Canada. Michael then went off the rails. He had violent eruptions and was verbally abusive to Deborah, much the same as he was to Theresa, but Theresa thought it sounded so much worse when it was directed at someone else. He began destroying the home, and they told him to leave. He never really took out his anger on Gary; in fact they hardly spoke to each other. Most of the abuse was centred on females.

Michael moved back home for a short period, and he completed high school with honours, but life for the family was stressful. Gary and Theresa had learned a lot from school and therapy while Michael was away, and this time they called a halt to the abuse and Michael moved out. Since then he has been involved in an abusive relationship with a young woman, which resulted in two separate changes of assault, and he has been charged with issuing death threats towards another young woman. He was drinking and doing drugs, hit bottom again and ended up in hospital twice in one week as a victim of street crimes. He has also been incarcerated for armed robbery. He continued to verbally abuse his mother, but she was now strong enough to put the phone down or throw him out of the house. He no longer stood confrontationally close because Theresa removed herself from the situation. Gary's daughters thought Theresa allowed him to treat her badly and that she gave him too much. She admits she did bail him out financially and with food, but thinks the girls do not understand what a mother feels for her child.

Over the years, Gary and Theresa have taken Michael to an endless list of therapists, counsellors and psychologists. The words, "There is no such thing as a problem child, just problem parenting," still ring in Theresa's ears. "How awfully cruel some therapists can be," she says. One therapist told them the problem was boredom and hyperactivity, and they should feed Michael a diet free of preservatives and colourants. This they followed diligently for three years. A psychologist asked them to look at a list of characteristics and pick out the ones they thought Michael possessed. He then told them they had a psychopath on their hands. A doctor said he had Attention Deficit Disorder (ADD) and prescribed Ritalin, but the drug left him in a fog, so he started to sell it.

Now Theresa realizes the abuse was far worse than she admitted at the time. She was ashamed and frightened of losing him to drugs and alcohol and now believes she enabled much of his bad behaviour. She carried around in her heart the fact that Michael witnessed her being abused when he was very young and used that as an excuse for her son's behaviour. The real crux of the matter, says Theresa, is where do you go to for help … *real help?*

*It's so hard. Being in the middle of a crisis in [this province] is like being in the desert with no water; you just know you are dying and no one is going to come and help you. The police tell you to call your doctor; the doctors put you on Prozac; the agencies and the hospitals all have huge waiting lists.*

## Donna

Donna was very happy when she became pregnant with Gabriella. She had had a number of miscarriages because of her husband's physical and sexual abuse, but she wanted to have a child. Donna thought she'd finally have somebody who would love her unconditionally, someone she could take care of and who would appreciate her care. She had no family around her and was totally alone. The church told her that if they had a child, her husband would mature and take more responsibility for his family.

But after Gabriella was born, the situation became worse. Donna had a second child, Crystal. At first Donna felt her baby was rejecting her, but soon learned that Crystal was hearing-impaired. If the children cried, their father would slap them and say, "There is something to cry about," and he would yell at Donna, "Shut them kids up."

Eventually Donna escaped, and the United Way helped her find a subsidized apartment to live in, medical help and assistance for milk for Gabriella. They were on their own for a couple of years but Crystal was anti-social and violent and Gabriella hyperactive. Donna found this extremely tiring. She saw a number of therapists but was not able to get any help, so she married again, thinking that a man might be able to get the girls to mind and that he would help around the house. This man was as abusive to Donna and the girls as was her previous husband, and she again escaped, this time to a women's shelter.

When the girls were five and six, Donna married her present husband, Phillip. For the next two years Donna was in and out of hospital being treated for post-traumatic stress disorder and severe depression. By 1997 Donna and Phillip could no longer look after the children, so child protection arranged for them to be fostered for a few months. The girls were traumatized. Crystal was extremely angry and frustrated because no one could understand what she wanted. She reverted to two-year old behaviour, began wiping bowel movements over the walls and peeing herself. She would not listen to any authority and would beat Donna until she was covered in bruises, scratches and bite marks. One day, Crystal beat her mother in public because Donna refused to buy an ice cream for her. Donna tried to tell the counsellors that something was wrong, but they said it was because Crystal was hearing-impaired and cranky. Donna said she knew hearing impairment doesn't give a child the reason to beat up people and there was something else going on. Crystal was just too violent. But Donna felt no one listened. She had few friends because of the girls' behaviour. Neighbours complained about Crystal's screaming. The church asked Donna not to bring the girls.

Crystal became severely depressed and even more violent but refused any treatment and was rude and uncooperative. At school she was beating other children and swearing at the teachers, and Donna received constant calls from the principal. At one point Crystal was not allowed on the school premises. The special education program in her school had refused to work with her, and the child welfare worker had no success. Crystal wrote notes to her parents saying, "I hate you. I am angry with you. I wish you were dead. I am going to kill you because you are mean." Donna's therapist and the child welfare worker said she should call the police, but the police had refused to respond in the past, so Donna took the girls to the police station. The officer told Donna, "Those kids are not intimidated by me at all. They have no respect for any authority figure. You've got a major problem on your hands."

Crystal thought about what the police officer said, she even cried on the way home. Gabriella had a tough-girl attitude and acted like it didn't bother her, but at summer camp she was beaten by another girl, heard about detention centres and prostitution, and saw how miserable the other teens' lives were. She witnessed a teenage boy get beaten so badly that his ear turned black. She was terrified. When she came home she talked about her experiences, and there was a change in her behaviour. She decided to finally accept help and go to a day treatment program. The worker made excellent progress with Gabriella, who accepted that she has anger issues and major self-esteem and self-confidence issues. She was diagnosed with Attention Deficit Hyperactivity Disorder (ADHD) and the medication seems to help.

The girls had destroyed their home and so the family recently moved to a new townhouse in the city. Phillip and Donna attended parenting sessions and are more together on parenting now. Donna says she has learned to use a more authoritative tone of voice to let the children know that they are frustrating or hurting her. Phillip is learning to have fun with the girls. Gabriella has made friends for the first time and is more confident that she can do her schoolwork. She still has her violent outbursts, but not as much. The school seems to understand the girls' situation and is able to work with them, and they make the girls take responsibility for their actions before they call Donna. That is a big burden off Donna's shoulders. Donna and Phillip even have visitors. They have had help with their parenting skills and family issues, and feel there is hope for the future. Gabriella is now fifteen and Crystal is fourteen. Both girls have been diagnosed with oppositional defiance disorder and fight with each other constantly. They continue to yell and scream and spit on their mother. Donna is exhausted, and said:

> *If I could do it all over again, I wouldn't have any children. I raised the girls in an extremely violent environment and they are the products of it. I selfishly wanted their unconditional love. Now I know that was a dream that could not come true. I have no idea what is going to happen to us.*

## Linda

Linda and Barry had dated for five years and were anxious to settle down and start a family. After three years, Richard was born, and two years later, the twins, Eli and Andrew. The strain and stresses of parenting three very small children took their toll, especially on Barry. He had difficulty handling the day-to-day responsibilities of being a husband and father, and there was increasing tension in the home. Linda worked full-time for the provincial government, and there were occasions when Barry, who worked part-time, looked after the children. But, in Linda's opinion, he didn't provide adequate care, and Richard was very aware of her concern. As early as four and five years of age, Richard was covering for his father to avoid tension.

When Richard was nine and the twins were seven, after years of Barry's verbal abuse and controlling behaviour, Barry and Linda separated. They attempted a reunion, but Barry became physically violent, and unfortunately, Richard witnessed the abuse. Linda and the children stayed at the battered women's shelter, then returned home. Barry went to live with his parents. Richard jumped into the role of substitute partner/father very quickly, and looking back, Linda realizes that she allowed this to happen. Richard became the person she would ask about what he and his brothers had done that day, who called and so on. It very quickly got out of hand. He became overprotective of Linda and expected her to account for her whereabouts at all times. If he and his brothers were in the care of a sitter, he would call her friends or work colleagues until he located her.

Linda tried to keep the communication open between Barry and the children, but he chose to distance himself from them. Invitations to school functions and church activities went unanswered. After a while Linda stopped expecting him to come, and so did Eli and Andrew. But not Richard, who tried to communicate with his father and to arrange visits between his father and his brothers. Because his father would not come to Richard, Richard went to him.

Even before his parents' separation, Richard had been aggressive and physical and would not accept responsibility for his behaviour. His behaviour worsened after the separation. The school suggested he attend counselling, and although Linda thought the behaviour was something he would outgrow, she did ask the family doctor for a referral. Richard saw the psychiatrist only once and refused to go back.

As a single parent with no family supports, Linda was isolated. Richard was physically aggressive towards his brothers, and his relationship with Linda deteriorated. He constantly put Linda down, called her names, defied her, listened in and taped her phone calls, went through her things and destroyed his brothers' belongings. Linda put locks on the bedroom doors and the phone under lock and key. She remembers locking herself and the twins in a bedroom while Richard raved outside the door all night. Their home life quickly became a living hell when Richard was present.

Linda sought the help of the family doctor who again referred Richard for counselling, but once again, he refused to attend. Eli and Andrew were scared of him, so Linda would never leave them alone. No one else witnessed these behaviours. In school Richard remained a good student and always helped others. At home the sitter noticed his aggressive behaviour, but in front of visitors or neighbours he was the "model child." It was Linda, Eli and Andrew who witnessed and suffered. Eli and Andrew were showing signs of stress because of the misery Richard inflicted on the family and were having trouble sleeping and problems in school.

Linda, who was trying to work, parent and rebuild her life, soon discovered that she could not count on any support from her colleagues or even close friends, because they thought her difficulties had to be caused by something she was doing. She worked hand in hand with service providers, but couldn't even talk to them about this. She felt guilty and a failure. The family suffered in silence.

In 1997 Linda began seeing the man who was to become her husband. Richard was twelve years old and increasingly verbally and physically abusive and threatening. The tension was unbearable and the family was sinking fast. Linda knew she had to do something. She describes the situation:

> *He left on Christmas Day amidst much cursing, screaming and throwing things, and I closed the door. His grandparents picked him up. Every chance he got that day he called my home with screaming and threatening. I was at my wit's end. It was then that I told him he could no longer live in our home. Either he had to be removed permanently or we were all going down with him. This was one of the hardest things I had ever done, but many harder things followed.*

Richard's father and grandparents welcomed him. At the time they simply felt that he was "misunderstood." In spite of her pain, Linda kept her distance, although she continued to meet with the school and kept "trying to fix things." Then, in September 1999, Richard's elderly grandfather called the police to have him removed from their home because he was physically and verbally abusing them. The police contacted Linda and told her they were bringing him home. She was shocked that they didn't even ask. The police officer, in Linda's words, "was not very nice." He repeatedly asked where he should take Richard. Linda felt very guilty. Her thirteen-year-old was at the police station, and she was refusing to have him home. He was taken to a residential centre.

Richard was diagnosed with conduct disorder and the majority of staff at the centre were very supportive, although others were judgmental of Linda. Since that time Richard has been to several counsellors and Linda went with him. He was in the temporary care of child welfare and they have been to court "countless" times. Linda visited Richard regularly and salvaged their relationship. She now hears "I love you Mom" every night instead of being cursed and get hugs rather than shoves. Richard is now sixteen and doing much better in school, but, after one unsuccessful attempt, has not slept overnight at home since he went to the centre. Linda saw how quickly things could revert to the horrible way it was. Richard maintains contact with his father, who has not seen Eli and Andrew in four years. Eli and Andrew have improved dramatically and are now self-confident honour students. They have regular contact with their brother, but are fearful that he will return home and disrupt their lives again. They accept that living under the same roof is not the only thing that constitutes a "family." Linda feels fortunate that the abuse has stopped, but she and her family have suffered a great deal.

On February 14, Linda's boss came to her office and told her there was a "handsome young man, bearing gifts" out in the hall. She couldn't imagine how Eli or Andrew could have found a ride into town but was curious and excited. To her surprise, it was Richard. He had a single rose and a beautiful Valentine's Day card for her. Linda said:

> *Knowing where we have been and what we have been through made this incredible. I realize that all situations are not as fortunate as ours and some may look and say, "Well, he is not at home, how can either of us be satisfied?" But after everything, the whole family knows that we took the right road — although it was rough. It was right for us. What a beautiful day it is here today.*

## Lori

Lori and her husband, Allan, have two children — Christopher, fifteen, and Melanie, eleven. Christopher had colic as a baby and cried constantly. As a small child, he was stubborn and would pinch and push Melanie, always bugging and teasing. Trying to stop him became an issue at home. He started getting into trouble at school in grade five, for minor things at first: acting out in class and pushing. When he was caught, he would flip out of control. Counsellors and psychiatrists now ask Lori why she didn't get help earlier, but when he was in grade five she didn't think anybody would have taken her seriously if she'd said, "I want to see a psychiatrist. My son pushed a child and then got a little crazy." By junior high, Christopher was repeatedly suspended from school for yelling at the teachers and calling them names. Eventually school couldn't deal with him any longer, and Lori tried home schooling. But that was a failure too.

Christopher began to steal, mostly things he didn't have any use for, like his sister's favourite stuffed animal, which he'd hide just to torture her. He didn't seem to care about anything and never showed remorse. If Lori sent him to his room he would follow her around the house, asking, "But why, but why, but why?" until Lori felt she was going out of her mind and would lock herself in her room to get away from him.

Over time, the abuse worsened. Christopher stole money from his parents, punched holes in the wall if they tried to discipline him and totally destroyed his bedroom. He broke into the garage and stole or ruined whatever he found. He lit posters on his wall on fire. One time, when he was grounded, Lori tried to stop him from going out, and he dragged her across the deck. In the end she let him go out. The police were constantly bringing him home for fighting and drinking, and he was charged with breaking and entering and possessing stolen property. He was also taking drugs. When his parents tried to talk to him, he would explode. Most of the time the family walked around on eggshells to avoid the abuse. Christopher would taunt Allan, "Come on, hit me!" Lori said, "I felt like saying, 'Hit him, just hit him.' It's ridiculous. It's just totally out of control." The family can no longer have family vacations because they can't take Christopher anywhere, and they can't ask anyone else to supervise him.

Lori got the brunt of the aggression because she was there most. She had days off work during the week and usually arrived home first. When the school called, she would be the one to leave work. But eventually Lori realized she couldn't do it alone any longer. It was too serious, too hard. She believes that if she hadn't had Allan with her, she would have "lost it" a long time ago. Allan actively supports Lori and attends the counselling appointments, but he feels bitter because of what the abuse has done to the family.

Christopher was diagnosed with oppositional defiant disorder, and Lori and Allan were told they had to be stricter, to set stronger guidelines and stick to them. So they did but to no effect. Lori thought the counsellor made it sound as if they didn't discipline him, and every time they left her office, Lori felt worse. The counsellor told them that they must never let Christopher get a rise out of them, so they always tried to be calm. But when they went back with Christopher to see her, he was really cocky with her and she did precisely what she had told Lori and Allan not to do: she got angry. Finally, the counsellor asked if she should close the file. Lori felt they'd had a diagnosis thrown at them, then shown the door. They didn't know what to do.

But the counselling did help Allan and Lori to see that Christopher was playing them off against each other, and they began to work better together. They turned to the police for help, but the police did not follow through on their promises of support. Lori finally did something she could never have imagined she would have to do: she called child welfare. But they couldn't help because he was fifteen and there was no place for him. They saw psychiatrists and counsellors but no one seemed to be able to do anything to help. The most support Lori received was from the school vice-principal who, she believes, understood. He told the psychiatrist and the police that this child needed help and that this was a priority case. Finally, Lori felt she had somebody on her side. But the most help she found was talking to other parents who have experienced abuse.

## Pauline

Pauline was married for eighteen years. She now admits that she and her husband, Ed, were doing a hard street drug, crack cocaine. Ed's father and grandfather were both abusive towards their families, and Ed had a destructive temper. Pauline fought back, and the children were exposed to a lot of pushing, shoving and verbal abuse. Ed also treated Pauline as if she were a child. Although Pauline insists that the children were always fed and cared for, she does admit that when they were high on drugs, she and Ed stole the children's possessions and sold them for drug money.

Pauline and Ed separated when Jeremy was twelve and Melissa thirteen. Jeremy had Attention Deficit Hyperactivity Disorder (ADHD) and Melissa had Attention Deficit Disorder (ADD) and suffered from depression. Melissa, like her father, refused to see a counsellor. Both teens took Dexedrine, and Pauline had to give them their medication because she suspected they would misuse it. She was the children's main caregiver and was mentally exhausted, terrified of being on her own and afraid to raise two teenagers. She was on medication for anxiety, which made her scared and paranoid, and Melissa started treating her the same way Ed had done: calling her names, and pushing and shoving her. After a few months, child protection intervened and the children went to live with their father. Pauline was distressed that the children were placed in the care of the man who had abused her. She was concerned that the child protection agencies offered no follow-up services, even when Ed asked for help. But it did give Pauline three months to get herself "back on track."

When the teens were visiting, Melissa was verbally abusive to her mother, especially when Pauline tried to tell her what to do. One day the abuse escalated and Melissa beat her mother. Pauline decided not to retaliate and Melissa returned to her father. Pauline didn't see her children for three weeks and found the separation from them extremely hard. Finally, Ed and Pauline talked to Melissa, told her that what she did was wrong and when she was with her mother she must obey her mother's rules. The children returned to live with Pauline.

Jeremy also defied his mother. He decided that nobody could boss him around, that he was a man now. He yelled at her, called her names, put her down like his father did, and threatened to put her head through the wall or to throw her out the window. Pauline didn't believe he would ever do these things and called it "stupid talk." Jeremy was also self-deprecating. He called himself stupid, put himself down, said that he didn't deserve to live and shouldn't be on this earth, and threatened to kill himself. Pauline knew that Jeremy needed counselling help, but she didn't know where to turn. The doctor suggested child welfare, but Pauline's experience had taught her that didn't work.

Pauline tried not to react when the teens were abusive and left the room rather than respond. Instead, she would ground them. On one occasion, Jeremy left the house without permission, and Pauline went and brought him home. Since that time, he has obeyed his curfews.

Pauline's concern was that her children get an education, and she struggled to get them to go to school and to stay in school. She worked closely with the schools and said it took a great deal of teamwork to get the children through. In spite of her efforts, Melissa was suspended.

Pauline has been off drugs for two years now, is back to work and feeling great. Once they came off drugs, they realized what was going on, and Ed began to support Pauline with the children. Now Ed has decided to move out of the province. Melissa, who continued to be abusive towards her mother, has decided to go with her father. Pauline is nervous about how she will cope without Ed's support, but she and Jeremy are now living with friends. They are good people who have lots of experience with having a normal, good family life and are helping Pauline and Jeremy to be a family. Pauline says that after all the years of craziness, this is wonderful. She believes the mistake she made was allowing herself to be hurt and intimidated by Melissa, and that has taught her a better way of reacting to her children. She doesn't know what is going to happen, but is confident they will get through it because they love each other and care very deeply if anything happens, even if on the surface, things don't always go right.

## Deborah

Deborah has been abused all her life. Her parents were young teens, and she was raised by an alcoholic grandmother. When Deborah was twelve, she was placed in a residential school for girls and has had little contact with her family since. She was abused at the centre and has received government compensation. She left school when she was sixteen with a grade-seven education, lived wherever she could find a place to sleep and had a baby that was taken by child protection.

Deborah now has two children — Jordan, who is fifteen, and Martin, seventeen. When the boys were little, she disciplined them with time-outs and sometimes a smack. By the time the boys were eleven years old, they began to smack her back, so she stopped doing that, but the boys continued to physically abuse their mother. A counsellor persuaded Deborah to call the police. Both her social worker and doctor assured her she had to do something to stop the abuse, but Deborah felt guilty about involving the police. Losing the boys was her fear. She didn't want them to go to jail, and she didn't want them to hate her. She loved her children with all her heart and soul and just wanted a normal life. Both boys were charged with assault. Jordan was incarcerated for three weeks and Deborah cried. Even though he was so abusive, she wanted him home. Jordan was also charged with an unrelated crime and was placed on house arrest.

The boys knew what buttons to push to make their mother cry. Deborah found it hard to cope and sometimes retaliated and threw things at the boys, other times she went outside to get away from the abuse. She felt as if the boys were the parents and she was the child. She was scared of her sons and tried not to get angry with them. The family had been evicted from numerous apartments because of the fighting and noise, so she was afraid to go out, even to school, because of what might happen while she was gone. She had a sign on her door stating, "Absolutely nobody is allowed in my home unless I'm home," but it was disregarded by the boys. When she protested, a fight erupted. Deborah tried to get them to understand that she was the mother and they the children, but they came and went as they pleased, cursed at her and pushed and hit her. Deborah once made them leave but was afraid what might happen to them on the street and begged them to return home.

Deborah felt helpless. Her husband, Wade, was an extremely abusive alcoholic who was on probation for assaulting Deborah. He had a destructive relationship with the boys, and once called Jordan, whose father is African Canadian, racist names. Jordan threatened him with a knife. Deborah was undecided about whether to continue the relationship with Wade.

Poverty was a constant struggle for Deborah. The last time she was evicted she had two children, a cat and their belongings in nine garbage bags. She had $700, no furniture, no blankets, nothing but their clothes and nowhere to go. She didn't know what she was going to do that day because it was pouring with rain. She was soaked, her cat was soaked and the children were soaked. They roamed the streets looking for a place until they finally found a landlord who took them in. It was December 13 when Deborah talked to us, and she had no money and nothing for Christmas. This was hard on Deborah and hard on the boys. She told them that they were lucky to have a roof over their heads and food on the table, because when she was their age she was living on the streets and fending for herself, but they were resentful and angry that their mother couldn't buy gifts or Christmas treats for them.

In the past she has worked as a cleaner and has also done volunteer work at a laundromat until it closed down. She was proud that they trusted her with the key and the moneybag. She had an opportunity to go back to school but found it too difficult, as she has a learning disability, which she believed was the result of all the beatings she had as a child. In addition, she was afraid of what the boys might do while she was out.

Deborah felt she had nothing to live for but her children. She knew she had to be there for them but they did not treat her with respect. She asked God why she was here and asked him to take her out of this world. She also knew she needed help with her past and with her current situation.

# 4.  Who Is Abused?

*It just makes me sad that she would do it. It broke my heart.*

When our children were teenagers, my friends and I used to share our parenting struggles. We all had problems, some more than others. Two of my friends were hit by their teens or were threatened or emotionally and financially abused, but at the time, it didn't occur to us that this was parent abuse. We didn't think of ourselves as abused parents.

In 1995, I started my research by looking for parents who would talk about their experiences of abuse. I asked fellow committee members to give my phone number to anyone they knew who was being abused by their teenagers and who would be willing to talk to me. Most people were surprised by the topic. They had never heard the term "parent abuse" and expressed disbelief and horror at the very idea. The counsellors and therapists had heard stories from their clients but had thought these were isolated incidents. After the meeting, a social worker came to me and in hushed tones told me her adolescent son was abusing her. We had served on this committee for a number of years, and I had no idea. In meetings after that, every time I raised the topic, someone would come forward as a victim or the friend or relative of a victim. Eventually, I was no longer surprised. Wherever I go, when people hear about my interest in parent abuse, they tell me about their own experiences or those of a friend or relative or co-worker. Recently, at a yard sale, a man was selling a book on parenting. When I told him I was doing research about teenagers who are violent towards their parents, he told me that was what he and his wife were going through with their daughter. The same thing happened with a staff member at the television station where I was doing an interview, a stranger on a plane, nodding acquaintances, even friends I thought I knew. What I came to understand is that we can never assume it isn't happening to people we know. So who are these parents who are being abused?

## Income, Ethnicity and Age

It is common for people to think that parent abuse occurs only in poor families. But research shows that this is not true. We interviewed women who work at home, women who work in a wide variety of workplaces, professional women and women who work at minimum wage, women who are financially comfortable and women who live on social assistance. Academic studies have conflicting findings about social class. Some studies find no relationship between parent abuse and poverty, others show more poverty in families where the teens are assaulting the parents, and yet others show higher rates of assault among middle- and upper-class families (Agnew and Huguley 1989; Charles 1986; Cornell and Gelles 1982; Eckstein 2002; Gallagher 2004; Paulson et al. 1990). Studies on delinquency show that there is a connection between disruptive school behaviour and petty crime on the one hand and social class on the other (Eccles and Barber 1999.; Hagan 1991; Lotz and Lee 1999). The implication is that the higher the social class a child comes from, the less likely they are to be disruptive at school or to be involved in petty crime. This may mean that the higher the social class, the less likely the children will be abusive, and by implication, parent abuse is more likely to occur in poorer families. But the connection is slight; the numbers are not dramatically different. We do know from our research that parent abuse is, in fact, found in all social classes.

Parent abuse, like all other forms of family violence, is also happening in most cultural and ethnic groups, although researchers note higher rates of assault among white families compared to black families (Agnew and Huguley 1989; Cazenave et al. 1979; Charles 1986; Cornell and Gelles 1982; Kumagai 1981; Omer 2000; Paulson et al. 1990). Immigrants are as vulnerable as any other parent, but they are faced with the additional challenge of helping their teens integrate into their new country while trying to encourage them to retain aspects of their own culture (Enang 2000: 7). Immigrant parents from Sudan and Guatemala, countries as far apart in culture as distance, have told me that in their countries of origin, girls live with their parents until they get married, at around twenty-five years old. In Canada, their teenage daughters control them by threatening to leave the family and "go and live in an apartment with friends." This is so appalling to them, they tolerate what they consider unacceptable behaviour to keep their teens in the family home. This control is not only the experience of Canadian immigrants. Haim Omer speaks of the eight-year-old son of a divorced Russian woman who, after living in Israel for only nine months, refused to speak to his mother in Russian. He mocked his mother, who could not speak Hebrew. She wanted him to fit in to his new country, and so she tolerated the abuse (2000: 75). Jerome Price in the United States, Eddie Gallagher in Australia and F. Kumagai in Japan have also written about parent abuse in their respective countries (Gallagher 2004; Kumagai 1981; Price 1996). Colleagues from Britain and South Africa tell me they see abused mothers in their daily work.

Another popular belief is that parent abuse is experienced primarily by people who became parents too young. However, in my 1995 parent abuse research study, the average age the parents interviewed began their families was in their late twenties. Academic researchers do not agree on the topic of age, but studies have shown that elderly parents of adolescents may be especially vulnerable to abuse (Kumagai 1981; Livingston 1986; Peek et al. 1985).

## "Permissive Parents"

The general public tends to think that parents are abused because they are too permissive. But what does the term "permissive" mean? If it means the parent listens to the teens, includes them in decision-making and allows them to make some of their own decisions, then this definition is problematic because, in families where the teen is not abusive, that would be considered good parenting. Many parents try hard to be fair and democratic, to give their children choices and to pay attention to the teens' opinions. This parenting style can be very successful and encourage teens to be independent and make their own wise decisions. Unfortunately it does not work with all teens. Trying to be an understanding and well-meaning parent, especially at a time when teens are beginning to feel physically more adult, can be difficult, and many parents avoid exercising authority. One of the first articles written about parent abuse suggested that this can result in "the adolescent's manifesting a grandiose sense of self along with an enormous sense of entitlement" (Harbin and Madden 1979: 1290).

The term "permissive" may mean inadequate or inconsistent rules and consequences, or absent parents. Often parents don't spend time with their teens, not because they don't want to but because they have to work. Parents also think teens have a right to their own time. In today's society, this may be taken to an extreme. Unsupervised time has increased dramatically for teens over the last forty years. According to one study (cited in the *Globe and Mail* 1999), by the time they are thirteen years old, almost a third of Canadian boys and a quarter of girls, spend five or more evenings a week out with their friends. Needless to say, teens would rather be out with their friends than home with their parents, and insisting they stay home can lead to family arguments that parents would rather avoid. Unfortunately, unsupervised time is related to a variety of non-acceptable teen behaviours.

Teens who have permissive or absent parents soon learn that anything goes, and there are few serious consequences for their behaviour. They suffer from low self-esteem and are as likely to develop conduct disorders as teens with more authoritarian parents. They also may believe that their parents don't care about them or don't have the time for them. When parents are not in control, teens may act out because they do not feel safe and may learn disrespect for their parents (Agnew and Huguley 1989; Charles 1986; Harbin and Madden 1979; Micucci 1995; Ney and Mulvihill 1982; Omer 2000).

Teens learn that by being abusive they can control their parents and get their demands met, but what they really want in many cases is attention. In her very readable book, *Reviving Ophelia: Saving the Selves of Adolescent Girls,* Mary Pipher offers examples of families where the children act out in a desperate attempt to get their parents to take control and give them a sense of security in the family. In families where teens are abusive, there is an even greater need for clear structure and leadership.

Many professional service providers believe that teens abuse their parents when rules are not clearly set down and enforced, and when boundaries are not clearly defined. By that they mean that parents need to know how to be in charge, to realize they have the right to set limits and to say, "This is my house and you can't behave that way in it." Most abused parents feel they do just that. They recognize that they carry ultimate responsibility and must have sufficient authority to prevent the child from causing harm to themselves or others. They try to set and enforce limits and sometimes are successful. But parenting is not always that simple. Most parents have tried to reason with their teens, but the teens can become even more abusive when their parents make it clear that the behaviour is unacceptable. It is difficult to know what to do when your child decides not to follow reasonable rules around things such as curfews or helping with housework, and it is precisely when the parents set limits or try to enforce them that problems arise and the abuse occurs. When parents physically try to stop grounded teens from going out or to get the teen to go somewhere they don't want to go, the teen often responds by pushing the parent away, sometimes violently. One mother said she was kicked in the head when she tried to get her daughter up for school. Knowing this, parents are too afraid to set limits. As one woman explained:

> *He would stand in the middle of the street and yell at me "You f—ing bitch, you can't f—ing make me do anything. I f—ing don't have to listen to you!" I would just close the door and go inside, thinking, you're right, what can I do? I was afraid of confrontations or arguments with him.*

The bond between parents and their children can be very intense, and parents are sometimes too frightened to insist on limits when their teens have threatened to withdraw their love or even themselves from the family. Few parents haven't felt a moment of sadness around their hearts when they heard their child say, "I don't love you anymore," or even "I hate you." One woman who lived with her daughter and grandchild was desperately afraid that her daughter would leave and take the baby, and she would never see them again. "Who would I hug if they left?" she asked. Other parents don't enforce limits because they feel guilty for things they did as parents or because they are trying to compensate for the inadequacies of the other parent.

Service providers, including teachers and police officers, believe that parents are more permissive because teens today have a greater sense of entitlement than did teens in the past. In other words, teens seem to feel that they deserve a good life, a well-paying job and brand-name clothes, not because they earned these privileges, but because it is their right. They also think they deserve their parents' services. Teens whose sense of entitlement outweighs their sense of responsibility can be in a very powerful position. These teens may care about little or nothing beyond themselves. Eddie Gallagher, a family therapist, psychologist and social worker with nearly thirty years experience working with families and young people in Australia, suggests it is, in fact, well-meaning parents who try too hard or attempt to be super-parents who:

> may produce children who expect to be entertained, who expect to be chauffeured about, who expect to be waited on, who even expect their home-work done for them! Many parents today (probably most of us) take responsibility for their children's education, entertainment and social life in a way that was rare even a generation ago…. It is easy to act abusively towards servants! (2004: 9)

Immigrants have pointed out that, unlike in their countries of origin, where family members value cooperation and contribution to the collective community, in Canada, there is more emphasis on the individual, and that can result in the teens becoming their mothers' equals (Enang 2000: 7). While it is problematic for teens to consider themselves their parents' equals, the approach has been successful. Only when the parents are abused does the finger get pointed at permissiveness as a cause. The term "permissive" should not be confused with neglectful or irresponsible parenting.

I hear people say that parents who are abused are not only permissive, they don't care about their children. This is simply nonsense. I have yet to meet an abused parent who doesn't care. At worst, they may have been inconsistent and not followed through with consequences for destructive behaviour. In my experience, parents who are not controlling their teens are not permissive but rather are showing the effects of being abused. They are too worn down by their teens' abuse to insist on obedience to the rules. Connie said that, looking back, perhaps she and her husband were not strict enough with their daughter. This was not because they didn't care, but because they were tired and frustrated, and it was easier to say yes than no when their guard was down. Most researchers in fact find that, rather than those who are overly permissive, parents who have used physical means to discipline their children are more likely to be victims (Cornell and Gelles 1982; Kratcoski 1984; Peek et al. 1985).

In contrast to "permissive" parents, "authoritarian" parents may use physically violent means and fear to try to control their teens. When the children were younger, during their early developmental stages, authoritarian parents saw their methods as "effective" because their children obeyed them. But for many, tension begins to surface as the child's need for autonomy increases and the parents try to maintain the same level of rigid control. The struggle intensifies as the teen, in an attempt to gain a sense of power in his or her life, becomes abusive. Studies show that rather than children whose parents are permissive, it is children who experience physical violence in the home who are more likely to grow up to be abusive. These teens are perhaps using violence as a way to stop their parents from hitting them, and in these cases it is overly-authoritarian or abusive parents, rather than permissive parents, who are being abused (Brezina 1999; Kratcoski 1982).

## Mother Abuse

Academic researchers agree that mothers receive the brunt of the abuse (Agnew and Huguley 1989; Cornell and Gelles 1982; Eckstein 2002; Evans and Warren-Sohlberg 1988; Gallagher 2004; Kratcoski 1982; Kumagai 1981; Livingston 1986; Pagelow 1989; Paulson et al. 1990; Salts et al. 1995; Wells 1987). My research confirms that women are the primary targets. As well as talking with friends and colleagues when I began this research, I put a notice in the local newspaper and talked on the radio requesting that abused parents talk with me about their experiences. Of the thirty-four parents who responded, thirty-three were women. Since then I have conducted further research and facilitated a number of public discussions of this topic. Without exception, significantly more women than men identify as victims, and both partners usually agree that the mother is more severely abused. Fathers and stepfathers can also be victims, but usually the abuse is less frequent and less severe. When violence occurs between teens and their fathers, fathers tend to perceive the incident as a fight rather than abuse.

Why women? One answer could be that many children are single-parented by their mothers. However, we should be cautious in accepting this explanation given the high levels of anxiety and moralizing that exist around family breakdown. To be sure, parent abuse is common among sole-parented children but this is because single parents are numerous. As many as half of all children under eighteen in North America will spend from a few months to years in single-parent households. More than half of the mothers in my research were single-parenting at the time of the interview and three-quarters had been single parents at one time, but not necessarily at the time of the abuse. Moreover, although there are academic studies that state that teen violence and anti-social behaviour are more frequent in single-parent families (Harbin and Madden 1979; Kumagai 1981; Livingston 1986), others state that assault is more common in two-parent families, or there is no difference (Charles 1986; Gallagher 2004; Peek et al. 1985).

It makes more sense, perhaps, to look at the role women play in their children's daily lives. Men, especially but not exclusively non-birth fathers, take relatively little or no part in the parenting. In the families we spoke with, there were fathers who were active parents, while others did little, if any, parenting, and a number were abusive towards their teenage children. Many women prefer that their intimate partners, especially those who are not the child's biological father, do not parent the children. Whether they are single-parented or not, or in families where parenting is shared, teens spend substantially more time with their mothers than their fathers.

As the mother has the most contact with the children, she also has most of the unpleasant contacts. Connie put it like this: "It seems that they lash out at the people who do the most for them, so mothers really bear the brunt of it." Teens have told their mothers that they vent their anger and frustration on her because she is the only other person present in the home. Fathers are simply not there as much to be abused. One teen, when asked why she abused her mother, said, "Because I have no one else." Even when they are physically present in a house, fathers are often emotionally absent. A psychologist who conducted detailed research showed that in a house where there was one problem child and one other sibling, the father's most frequent activity was reading the newspaper, while the mother had as many as one unpleasant interaction with a child per minute (Patterson 1980). Fathers' involvement with their children may be changing with the times, but not enough to significantly alter the statistics.

This raises the question of whether abuse is more prevalent when mothers can't depend on fathers to support/provide discipline. Traditionally, fathers were the disciplinarians; they set the rules, defined the boundaries and made sure there were consequences. Today, it would appear, this is no longer the case. In my research, even when fathers were present, mothers were usually more responsible for setting the limits and administering consequences for broken rules. One woman explained: "Their father really didn't pay attention to the children unless they were noisy. They could be children until he drove in the driveway, then they had to be like little adults." She was the one who decided on the rules and carried out the punishments. Women told us they prefer to do the disciplining in the family because they do not trust their male partner's ability to do it. They believe that men are more likely to respond aggressively and go too far when punishing their children, and many are afraid that they too will be abused when they try to intervene. Theresa's husband, who was very controlling and had an unpredictable temper, had little contact with their son, but when he did, the two would physically fight, and Theresa would be abused when she tried to separate them. One teen told us that she grew up with an angry father who would "scream and yell a lot … hit walls and put holes through them." One day her mother tried to stop her father "going upstairs after me and my brother. I guess she fell backwards down the stairs. I thought he pushed her and I went nuts." Connie told us her husband "did pretty well," but the abuse took an awful toll on him and he just didn't know how to handle it. Connie could see that her husband and daughter both had hot tempers, and she lived in fear that "something would happen."

Mothers often have a closer emotional connection to their children. Many teens agree that it is easier to share their emotions with their mothers and they're not as afraid of their mothers as they are of their fathers. Consequently, teens tend to talk to their mothers more than to their fathers. By the same token, mothers are perceived as being "softer" than fathers and are, therefore, easier targets for abuse. Society in general is more comfortable with anger directed at women than at men (Bass and Davis 1988). Teens told us they would never dare hit their strong and intimidating fathers: "I'm scared of my father. He's bigger and stronger than me," and "It's a male thing: we're all scareder of men. Dads say, 'Do it. I mean it. Do it now,' and you do. Moms are a pushover." Connie agrees. She believes it's usually the mother that teens hit because they know their mothers won't hit them back, and they don't know that about their fathers:

> *It's usually the mother that they hit because they know that they are going to get away with it or Mom isn't going to hit back. She knew that if she did something to her father, she would probably get a good crack. It's a terrible thing to say, but she couldn't beat him up and she could beat me up. I think that, being the mother, I was always a bit more lenient with her than her father. I'd always give her another chance, and her father wanted to kick her out.*

Theresa told me that David never really took out his anger on her husband, that in fact they hardly spoke to each other, other than when her husband told him to leave the house. Teens also say they would rather be nasty with their mothers than their friends because:

> *You can get over a fight with your mom quicker than with anyone else. If you fight with a friend you don't talk for a long time. Teens take their parents for granted. They take out their aggression on their parents because parents will forgive them.*

Teens expect to be able to talk to their mothers and may be outraged when there are difficulties. One mother told us her daughter, "says I'm too soft-hearted, I'm always crying, and she can't tell me anything because I'm always crying." Teens even try to get their mothers to be aggressive. The mother's passivity may well be the best strategy she has for protecting herself at that time. One mother said, "He actually wanted to provoke me so that I would hit him." But many women, like the one whose daughter yelled at her constantly with, "Who do you think you are? You're nothing," say they cannot respond: "I'd been a doormat so long that they just repeated what they heard. I'd say, 'That's not nice, don't say that,' but that's all I'd do." A teen's physical size and greater strength can intimidate their mothers (Agnew and Huguley 1989; Harbin and Madden 1979; Kumagai 1981; Paulson et al. 1990), although mothers who are physically larger than their teens also experience abuse, as this mother explained: "I'm not a fighter although I'm bigger than her, I'm not aggressive with her. I would try to get her hands away from my neck when she was choking me, but I won't get angry with her."

The deep emotional connection mothers have with their children has been documented and studied by researchers. As one service provider said, "We can separate ourselves from another adult, but children are our flesh. We protect our children even when they victimize us." Mothers know they have difficulty separating themselves enough to see clearly: "For a mother, taking care of yourself as a person and seeing it as separate from the care of your children is difficult, because you're so enmeshed with your child, especially as a single parent." Theresa loved the deep and special emotional bond she had with her son, but now recognizes she allowed David to be her friend, her father, her brother. She wonders if the relationship was too close, and perhaps unhealthy, because their closeness was tinged with her guilt about allowing her son to witness her dysfunctional marriage and for leaving him with a caregiver while she worked to support them. Another mother said:

*What made me so sad was this was a little girl I'd take shopping on Saturday — we wouldn't spend money, just look. We'd laugh and talk and dream together. I thought we were such good friends. I think I was really hurt she took all those dreams away. And she didn't even understand what she'd done. There was nothing she could do to stop me loving her. There's no way in the world I would let anyone else do to me what she did, but you do it for love. You're afraid you'll lose that love. I think I do love her, but I'm scared to let her know because I don't know what she'll do with that.*

Even when their children are abusing them, parents, particularly mothers, feel the need to take care of their children, both emotionally and physically. Abused mothers continue to cook their teens' meals and do their laundry and care about the teens' well-being. In spite of being severely physically and mentally abused by her son, Sarah, whose story was told in Chapter Two, is more concerned about him than she is about herself. Her greatest fear is that he will hurt her seriously, or even kill her, and he'd have to live with that for the rest of his life. Lori said she felt helpless and scared for Christopher, and worried that he would "end up in jail. Or wind up dead." Pauline blames herself for allowing her daughter to assault her, and says, "I shouldn't have let her beat on me because I knew it had to be really hurting her, what she did to her mom." When the police arrested Irene's son for abusing her, Irene's concern was that he didn't take his coat and might be cold.

Recent evidence indicates that this may be chemical as well as emotional. One group of academics suggests that women respond to stress differently than men. In stressful situations, men tend to have a "fight or flight" reaction, that is, they feel more comfortable hitting out or separating from others. Women respond to stress with a cascade of a brain chemical called oxytocin that:

> encourages her to tend children and gather with other women instead. When she actually engages in this tending or befriending, studies suggest that more oxytocin is released, which further counters stress and produces a calming effect. This calming response does not occur in men, because testosterone which men produce in high levels when they're under stress seems to reduce the effects of oxytocin. Estrogen seems to enhance it. (Taylor et al. 2000)

The article further states that the vast majority of subjects in stress research have been males, and it was thought that women's reaction to stress was the same as men's. This research finding has implications for parent abuse. It would follow that when fathers are stressed by their adolescents, their reaction is to respond as aggressively as the child or to separate from the child. The mother's reaction is to try to get closer to the child. This may explain why mothers so strongly resist separating from abusive children and experience intense pain when they do. In addition to being worried about their child's safety, the separation may trigger a chemical conflict in the mother. Because of this close bond, mothers protect their children even when being victimized by them and may be less able than fathers to take a stand and give the ultimatum to follow the rules or leave the house. This, however, is not always the case. One couple told me that the father was adamant that his son, however violent, belonged with them, and the mother eventually left. Although this father recognized the damage his son was doing to the family and that, with this level of violence, they could not all live under the same roof, he could not bring himself to give up on his boy. Eventually, after eighteen months, the father admitted his mistake, the boy left the home and the mother returned. Another couple talked about the financial abuse they were experiencing, and both agreed that while the mother was consistent and abided strictly by the rules, the father did not. He was "the softy."

Many women who are being abused by their teenage children have also been the victims of abuse by an intimate partner (Carlson 1990; Gallagher 2004; Jaffe et al. 1990; Pottie Bunge and Locke 2000; Reuter and Conger 1995; Simons et al. 1995). According to Statistics Canada, 51 percent of Canadian women have experienced at least one incident of physical or sexual assault since the age of sixteen. Children are exposed to this violence. It is interesting that teens don't always respond with violence towards the person who hurt them or hurt their mother, but by abusing the person they see as the least powerful. I rarely hear of cases where teens use aggression against an abusive adult male in an effort to protect the mother. Instead, they focus their retaliation on their non-abusive parent, so the victims of spousal abuse may also be victimized by their children.

Sometimes, it is when the woman leaves her abusive partner (Gallagher 2004) that the children begin to abuse her. Richard witnessed Linda being verbally abused and assaulted by his father. Jordan, who has assaulted his mother, says being abused by his mother's partners and watching these men abuse his mother was typical in his home. Women learn submission as a response to violence:

> There has always been abuse in my family as far back as I know. Our grandfather was abusive to my grandmother. My father was an alcoholic and was emotionally and verbally abusive to my mother and us. I never remember my mother being abusive to us, just supportive, kind of a doormat.

When women feel guilty about the abuse their teens were exposed to, they frequently blame themselves for the abuse they are now suffering from the teens:

> *My husband was physically abusive towards me, he's alcoholic, and he was physically abusive towards [our daughter]. I think if I hadn't put up with all his abuse for all those years she wouldn't be as bad as she is.*

One woman told me that, in our society, it is the mother's job to keep the peace and make sure the family is a happy one, and if she is being abused, she is not doing a good job. Donna takes responsibility for the effect that a violent home had on her daughters. She was the victim of abuse from more than one intimate partner, and now her girls are abusive towards her. Another mother who was abused by her partner told me that her teenage daughter contemptuously yelled at her, "You're nothing but a coward!" One mother told us her daughter thinks she's weak, but she says she didn't fight back with her abusive husband and she won't do it with her daughter. For many years Theresa excused her son's abusive behaviour because she felt guilty about the violence he had been exposed to when he was very little:

> *Naturally I have always carried this fact around in my heart — bad mom, bad upbringing stuff — and honestly I have used this as an excuse for my son's recalcitrant behaviour on many occasions. By the time my head was straight it was obvious that I had a very difficult child on my hands.*

Gallagher believes that women abused by their partners "create high levels of entitlement in their children" because they are trying to "make up for 'depriving' their children of their fathers and for exposing them to [domestic violence]" (Gallagher 2004).

More than a few women have been abused all their lives. This debilitates them and the family gets caught in a cycle of abuse. Deborah, who had been abused as a child and later by her partners, was eventually abused by both her sons. Jordan, who was fifteen years old and on probation for assaulting her when we spoke with him, had seen Deborah being physically and emotionally abused by her boyfriend, Wade. He shows little respect for his mother and says, "My mother can't take care of herself." Women who are abused by their partners deal with multiple stresses. Theresa's son, David, suffered from colic and chronic ear infections. The baby was very demanding, and her abusive husband "physically took it out on me if the baby cried too long."

The cycle of violence affects not only women. Men who have been abused as children are also vulnerable to abuse from their teens. Donna's current husband, Phillip, is struggling to be a good stepfather to Donna's extremely abusive daughters, but at times he has handled the situation badly. Searching for the love he didn't get from his parents left Phillip unable to adequately parent:

*A lot of this has to do with my upbringing. My dad was physically and mentally abusive to me. He's long since stopped drinking but he was an alcoholic. When he was drinking, we would get the belt or whatever was close by that he could get his hands on. He used his fists and left physical marks on me. I have scars on my forehead and my chin. It wasn't until I started seeing the psychologist that I understood the connection with the way I was treated as a child, and the kids treating me like trash now. I wanted love from my mom and dad when I was a kid, and I didn't get it so I kept searching for something I couldn't have. I hurt everybody in the process. But it's over now.*

## Parental Conflict

Another major area of vulnerability is parental conflict. Parents who are not getting along together are especially likely to be the targets of abuse (Omer 2000; Price 1996). Although it usually helps to have more than one adult in the home (Dornbusch et al. 1985), couples who aren't working together can make the situation worse. As Omer put it, "Marital war can be worse than aloneness" (Omer 2000: 60). Dealing with an abusive child can limit the amount of quality time adults are able to spend together, leaving them inadequate space to work on their own relationship. It becomes a vicious cycle when their conflict with each other saps the time and energy they could be spending with their children and detracts them from working together to deal with the abusive teen. Abusive teens can deepen these marital problems and can disrupt the entire family. One mother said her daughter caused difficulties between her parents by telling "her father I'd done things to her.... My husband believed her. She was his baby." Another mother said: "We were starting to have marital problems and I was also concerned for my other children, for my sanity. My entire life was being torn apart because of one individual." Lori and her husband, Allan, are hanging in together, but the abuse is having a destructive effect on their relationship:

*We've been through so much. We've tried to get help and we've tried to help our son, and Allan's just tired. We're both tired. We've stuck together, and we still have quite a good relationship. We get up every morning and talk about what's going on and I still tell him everything I'm doing. But we don't have time for the closeness we once had anymore, so it's driving us apart that way. I worry about it but I just figure that at some point we'll come back together. Right now, there's just no time for us anymore. We're together about Christopher, but as far as time to have fun or to go places, no.*

Occasionally parents actually encourage the abuse by using the teen as a weapon to hurt the other parent. When parents fight, or when children are exposed to parents being abusive towards each other, the children learn that abuse and violence are acceptable in their homes.

Parents who get along well with each other but have different parenting styles may find their relationship torn apart by the consequences and may be leaving themselves open to abuse. This can happen, for example, when one parent attempts to set clear boundaries and consequences which are contradicted by the other parent. This gives the children conflicting messages and they tend to react in one of two ways. They become very resentful towards the "authoritative" parent and challenge the rules because "Dad (or Mom) says I don't have to," a dynamic openly or secretly supported by the "permissive" parent. Or they use abusive behaviour as a means to threaten or intimidate the "permissive" parent into altering certain rules or boundaries that had been established by the "authoritative" parent. In both scenarios, the teens' behaviour stems from the fact that the parenting styles differ. This mother was abused when she tried to impose standards that contradicted those of the teen's father:

*How do you explain to a child that her father was spoiling and controlling her and he was someone I wouldn't want her to be with? How do you explain that you want them to be protected from someone you'd originally taught them to love? You want them to love and respect their father but at the same time you don't want them to be like that. He let her be very sassy to him and I wouldn't let her talk to him that way in my house.*

Linda and Barry are a typical example of a couple whose inability to work together may have contributed to the abuse. Linda thinks, as a result of the increasing conflicts with Barry, she unintentionally allowed Richard to assume a caregiver role in the family, a role for which he was far too young. Linda agrees that if she and Barry had been able to work together better, Richard would not have been as abusive.

Abusive teens consume a great deal of parents' attention and leave them with less time and energy to spend on maintaining a healthy relationship with each other. In turn, conflict with each other means they have less time and energy to spend on their teens. Over time, the increased cycle of conflict and alienation between the parents makes it more difficult for them to respond effectively when the teen is abusive. Friction can result when parents don't agree that the behaviour is abusive, but whether they agree or not, it may be difficult for one parent to know how to support the other. One father said he just didn't know what to do when he saw his wife being abused by their daughter:

> *It drove a wedge between my wife and me. I had to decide between being a father to my children or a husband to my wife. It was impossible to see my child as the culprit — she was always quiet and docile when I came home, and it was my wife that was "freaking out."*

When separation or divorce is not amicable, parents sometimes use the children to hurt each other, and this makes the abuse worse. In his therapy practice, Price (1996) sees many more children of divorced parents than children of parents who are together. He believes this is because divorce is often adversarial in our society, and nasty, angry divorces typically create stress for teens. After Linda and Barry separated, Barry had little contact with Linda or the children, and nine-year-old Richard resented Linda for this. The paternal role Richard had begun to assume before the separation worsened and soon became abusive. Karena thinks that her abusiveness towards her parents was a reaction to a cycle of abuse resulting from her parents' problems, especially when they divorced.

In families where parents have separated, the children sometimes blame the parent they live with (usually the mother) for changing their home, community, school, friends and lifestyle. Karena was used to taking care of her little sister, and when she moved out of her mother's home and went to live with her father, she no longer had responsibility to anyone but herself, and she did not like the change. One mother told us she was reduced to poverty because her husband refused to send child-support, and the teens resented her for it. This mother is caught in a vicious cycle: the teens express their anger in abusive behaviour, and in an attempt to stop it, she spends her time running from one social and justice agency to another. No employer would give her the time off to do this, so she can't work and remains poor. Teenagers are sometimes jealous of the loss of attention from their mother or father when new partners become involved. The situation is intensified when new partners brings their children with them. In her story, Theresa describes David's resentment at having to adjust to their new family.

Whether they are living together or not, parenting is less fractious when parents agree on a parenting style. As children on average spend far more time with their mothers than their fathers, it is usually mothers who have to impose consequences for the child's behaviour. It stands to reason, then, that it is important that mothers have support from the children's fathers to do this vital work. Instead, irresponsible fathers can sabotage the mother who is trying to do the best for her children. They do this by being nasty to her in front of the children, or behind her back, by mucking up access arrangements and withholding support payments.

When their parents abuse each other or fight, children learn that abuse and violence are acceptable ways of dealing with difficulties. Studies show that children whose parents get along well have fewer behavioural difficulties than those whose parents are in conflictual marital situations (Omer 2000; Shulman and Seiffge-Krenke 1997).

## Siblings, Relatives and Pets

Abusive teens may also strike out at less powerful members of the family, such as younger siblings or pets, adding to the parents' stress. In families with abusive teens, more often than not the other children are not abusive. Connie, for instance, has two daughters, but only one is abusive, and Linda has two non-abusive sons. Parents fear for the physical and emotional safety of their other children, worrying that they will also be abused or will see the abusive behaviour and copy it.

Linda's story illustrates the impact on siblings. Linda's twin sons suffered not only verbal abuse at the hands of their nine-year-old brother, Richard, but also physical abuse. Eli and Andrew began showing signs of stress. The twins both had a speech impairment since birth which worsened, and they began having trouble sleeping and problems in school. Lori is also distressed about the effect of Christopher's behaviour on his sister, Melanie. Lori explained:

*He doesn't bug his sister any more. He comes home stoned all the time and can't be bothered with her. It's a sin, because she looks up to him. She sticks up for him and runs to his defence when he's in trouble. She'll tell me she was there and it wasn't Christopher's fault. It is odd that she does that because of all he's put her through. She is really emotional. When they fight, she cries and gets migraines. I've had to take her and lie down with her, put a cold cloth on her head. It just makes me so angry that he does this to our family. I don't want Melanie to go through this. I don't want our family to be upset.*

Observing the teen's dangerous activities, particularly those involving drugs, alcohol and prostitution, is dangerous for the siblings and a constant worry for the parents. One dynamic is for the other children to act out in order to get attention, and another is for them to become depressed because the entire family focus is on the abusive teen. Their parents are left with little time and energy to pay positive attention to them. Connie realizes that Emily's behaviour affected the entire family. Her daughters were very close, and Emily's sister tried hard at the beginning to help her but eventually gave up.

The abuse of a parent can be extremely painful for a sibling. Sometimes the siblings get so disgusted with what is going on at home that they leave at the first opportunity, adding a further layer of anxiety and sadness for the parents. Bonnie is now thirty-five years old. Her older brother, Tim, has been controlling his mother since he was ten years old. She knows what is happening, she sees her mother's suffering and inability to act, but doesn't know how to help. It is a constant pain in her heart and tears roll down Bonnie's face when she talks about the situation at home. She knows she cannot change her mother or her brother and feels the situation has damaged her.

Frequently, parents find that the teen's abusive behaviour leads to arguments or tension between them and other adult members of the family or friends, especially when teens attempt to manipulate others into believing the abuse is the parents' fault. One parent said her daughter would call her father, aunt and grandmother and tell them stories and lies. If the family or friend sides with the teen, relationships are jeopardized and can be damaged. Social opportunities are curtailed because people don't want to be around children who misbehave. The message Theresa received from her friends was, "Come for tea, but please don't bring David." Abused parents are likely to have trouble with neighbours who are disturbed by the violence. Donna receives constant complaints about Crystal's screaming. The neighbours accuse her of not knowing how to look after her children.

## The Common Despair

Connie, Donna, Linda and the other parents who are abused come from all walks of life and practise a wide variety of parenting styles. There is no single or simple profile of an abused parent. However, they do have one thing in common. It is not their age or culture or income level or their ability to be good parents. It is their despair. They feel hopeless, helpless and in emotional turmoil because they are unable to control the situation and because of the possible physical danger. These are parents who have lost their leadership role in their families and are shocked that this could happen. The despair feeds on itself. When parents are feeling confused, helpless, hopeless and guilty, they become unsure of themselves and are less able to handle a situation that requires strength and fortitude. Their inner resources become so eroded that they are less and less able to take control. When Connie's daughter assaulted her, and Connie was crying and hurt, a passerby called the police. She described her despair at not being in control of the situation, because involving the police "was probably the last thing in the world I wanted to happen, but I wasn't thinking straight." This mother clearly felt out of control in relation to her daughter:

> She'd bring her boyfriends home and have sex with them. Some of them had criminal records. She used foul language and physical threats. She physically fought us. She threatened to lay charges against me and I'd say, "Go ahead, I'd be safe behind bars. I'll be able to get away from this.

Another commonality is that the victims of parent abuse carry the burden of public blame and shame (Ambert 1992; Caplan 1989). When teens behave badly we immediately blame the parents. We think, "Where are the parents? What have the parents done wrong?" And by parents we usually mean mother. Knowing this, Lori protested, "There is absolutely nothing wrong with our family. Christopher comes from a good home where we've been together forever. We don't do drugs, we're not alcoholics." She says she's scared to even have a drink in case something happens and she has to run out and drive the car, or the police have to come and they'll think, "Oh, no wonder he's like that."

Women live under the threat of not meeting societal expectations of being good mothers. The children know their mother's fear of being condemned as bad mothers, and they intentionally hurt them with comments like, "It's your fault I'm like this because of the way you brought me up." The fear of this condemnation also encourages parents to keep the abuse secret. They blame themselves for not being able to produce a happy family, they question their parenting abilities, agonize over where they went wrong and feel like failures. One mother said, "I feel punished. It's like all the mistakes I made in parenting have come back to haunt me."

Parents also feel unsupported and isolated. Connie says no one understood. Even her other daughter, Joanne, thought she was crazy to put up with the abuse. The result was that she had nowhere to turn. She suffered alone, couldn't sleep or eat and became depressed. Linda suffered alone too. Only she and her other children knew about the abuse and they kept it secret. She remembers with horror the screaming and crying when she and her sons locked themselves in a bedroom for an entire night while Richard ranted and raved outside the door. But no one else witnessed these behaviours. In school Richard remained a good and helpful student; in front of visitors and neighbours he was "the model child." Donna and Phillip were also isolated by their children's behaviour. They felt they couldn't invite friends to their house because the children had trashed it.

All abused parents have made mistakes. Parents can see their mistakes and acknowledge their responsibility, but don't know what to do, or they think they may have made mistakes but can't quite put their finger on what caused the abuse. Connie said, "I'm sure I made mistakes and there are probably things that I did and said that I shouldn't have, but at the time you don't really know. I questioned myself till I drove myself crazy." Lori said she constantly thinks of all the things that maybe she could have done differently:

*Maybe I shouldn't have worked full-time. We were always rushing. We didn't have time to enjoy him when he was a baby, even though he was very hard to enjoy because he had colic and cried all the time. I felt I was going mad. We weren't doing as well as we're doing now. Everything was a struggle. This little baby was just put in the middle of it and it put a strain on all of us. Maybe Christopher felt that as a baby. I don't know. It bothers me to think that maybe that's why he's the way he is today.*

The truth is that whether they are abused or not, all parents make mistakes. Omer quotes a writer who says that parents' human flaws are, paradoxically, essential to a child's development. He says, "Indeed, if the mother were perfectly attuned to the child's needs, the child would not thrive" (Omer 2000: 28). Unfortunately, our society has set up an ideal of the perfect mother, one whose house is always clean and who is always there for her perfectly behaved children, who are doing well in school. None of us reaches the ideal. Obviously, it is important that we don't damage our children, but our honest best should be good enough.

Another thing abused parents have in common is that they feel, with good reason, that they are unable to trust their teen. This understandably leads to difficult situations. One teen lied so often that when she was in trouble at school, her mother found it difficult to support her. Lori said she initially used to run to Christopher's defence when people talked about him. She would think, "not my son." But she "usually wound up looking like a fool when the truth came out. It was so hard to believe." The result is that now she finds it very hard to defend him. Crystal was so disruptive that her parents could not leave her unsupervised at home. They couldn't take her with them, even to church, but knew of no one who would supervise her. If they go out, the uncertainty of what will confront them when they return is always on the parents' minds. Lori says, "It's like my son controls everything we do. We can't do anything really. We can go to work and come home, and that's it." Parents don't know if the teen will be home when they return or if their home and possessions will be damaged. One mother told me she was glad to go to work and get away from the abuse, and she would dread coming home; her first fear was that her daughter wouldn't be home, and her second fear was that she would be. She said, "I'd go home on the bus worrying about what she'd do to hurt me tonight." Because they can't trust their teens unsupervised at home, their social life becomes limited. One mother, for example, called home twice during an interview with us to check on her teens. Another said, "I have no social life and can't have a relationship because supervising her takes up all of my time. It's been too hard to go to support meetings because I can't leave her home alone."

Parents told us they thought it was only a matter of time before their child would badly beat or kill them. One mother described her daughter as "a walking time bomb," as she never knows what to expect from her and is constantly waiting to see what she'll do next: "I'm scared she'll get mad at me one day and she'll pick up a knife and that'll be the end." When parents are this afraid of their children, they feel they have to be on guard all the time and even lock their bedroom doors. One mother said she "tip-toes" around her daughter and is careful not to ask too many questions about her daughter's friends, or where she is going, because she knows "what triggers her."

The stress of dealing with an abusive teen can have a negative impact on parents' health, making existing health problems worse or causing new ones. A high number suffer from stress-related disorders and lack of sleep. Despair alone can make people physically ill. A number of parents told us that they used prescribed medication to help them deal with the tension and stress of the situation. Yet medication can cause even more problems. Irene said that during the abusive times she felt physically ill and added, "I felt like I was dying." She had pains in her stomach and head and was severely depressed. The doctor prescribed sleeping pills, but they made her sluggish. One mother developed nervous bowels and had to take tranquilizers. The lack of control of her life makes her feel that she is not "the same person I was two years ago." And another mother said she wasn't coping emotionally, couldn't sleep or eat and became depressed, took sleeping pills and "wasn't in good shape for myself or anybody else." She wonders now how she survived. Stress and lack of sleep affected one mother's health so much that she took sleeping pills and had to make regular visits to the doctor. In situations such as these, parents may also turn to alcohol or illegal drugs to help them cope.

Problems at home spill over into the workplace since parents take their anxiety with them. Concern about where the child is, if they are getting into trouble or are in danger interferes with the parents' concentration on their work and leads to additional anxiety about the security of their job. Parents worry about the number of phone calls they receive at work concerning their teenager, as well as the amount of time they have to take off to deal with emergency situations or court appearances. They are often exhausted and worry that will affect their work. One mother said:

> She stays out all night and doesn't phone. She'll leave her house keys at home and then when she decides to come home in the middle of the night she wakes me up by yelling to me to let her in. It disrupts my sleep and I have to get up in the morning and go to work.

Parents, especially those who are supporting their families, worry about losing their jobs. The cost of counselling the family when public services are inadequate or unavailable adds a financial strain that makes it even more imperative that parents remain employed.

## Conclusion

Parent abuse is far from a rare occurrence in Canada today, but it is such a well-hidden form of family violence that it could be happening to our relatives, friends and co-workers without us knowing it. The women we talked to found it extremely difficult to admit to themselves that their child would hurt them and to move to the next step of naming the child's behaviour as abuse. It was even far harder for them to talk about it to others. It was their despair and desperation for help, as well as their desire to help others who are equally isolated, that drove them to find the courage to talk to us about their families. They knew that the idea was so abhorrent that they might be met with disbelief and blame. I have tremendous respect for these women and feel privileged to have heard their stories.

The stories proved to me that there is no such thing as a typical abused parent. They were comfortably off financially and poor, home-makers and with jobs in the workplace, single parents and with partners. They came from many different backgrounds, but most were main-stream Canadians. I am currently conducting research to find out whether immigrants' experiences in Canada contribute to the abuse they experi-ence or if their teens were just as abusive in their countries of origin.

The women who told me their stories had done their best in a world that is not always good to mothers and doesn't always understand the deep emotional connection mothers have to their children, a world that blames them for their children's behaviour before it offers support. They had tried to be fair, to listen to their children and pay attention to their needs. A few realized they had been too severe with the children, others that they had been overly permissive. It was clearly difficult for them to gauge exactly what kind of parenting the child needed, especially when the other children in the family responded well to the style of parenting they had chosen. They were pressured by today's societal norm that dictates that teens shouldn't have to spend time with their parents and that parents shouldn't interfere in their teens' lives. Spending time with the teen was unpleasant and led to arguments, so I think it is understand-able that eventually the parents gave up trying.

These women taught me that what they have in common is the extreme stress they suffer, and that they all feel guilty, isolated and unsupported. They questioned their parenting abilities, agonized over whether or where they went wrong and felt responsible, without hope and helpless. They felt they had failed. I can sympathize with their feelings. When my daughter was a teenager we had our struggles. It was far from easy, and there were many occasions when I worried about how good a mother I was. At times I felt like crying or screaming and behaved less well than a sensible adult should. But like these mothers, I continued to love my child and clung to the belief that she would turn out well. Fortunately, she is now a loving adult herself. The mothers we talked to continue to love their children and cling to rays of hope. As much as Christopher is out of control, Lori says that every now and then she sees a little something in his eyes that suggests maybe he does want help:

> *When we're alone, like if we're driving home from psychiatrists and we're talking, I can see his eyes fill up and I think, there is still something good in there and I just can't bring it out. Then he gets back with all his friends, and it's gone. I've lost him again.*

We will now look at what the teens themselves say. This book is about parents, and the vast majority of our interviews were with parents and service providers, but it is also valuable to hear how teens perceive the abuse.

# 5. Teens Speak

Finding teens to interview was difficult. Only three of the children of mothers we interviewed — Deborah's son, Jordan, and Donna's daughters, Crystal and Gabriella, agreed to be interviewed. Deborah and Donna's stories are in this book. A number of organizations like teen health centres and youth centres knew of teens who were abusing their parents and suggested that they talk with us, but few agreed. I have chosen to include here three stories from teens who physically abused their parents. The stories from Jordan, Crystal and Karena were chosen because they most clearly articulated the teens' feelings about the abuse.

## Jordan

I am fifteen and I'm under house arrest. And it sucks. I can't do anything. There's no freedom. I want to go out with my friends and play basketball. Go work out. I have good friends but my mother doesn't like them hanging around the building because we used to smoke weed.

I started doing drugs in school but then I was expelled for being too disruptive in class. The teachers and the kids just bugged me all the time. Certain teachers would say something and I'd get right mad and then I'd just say the wrong thing and I'd get kicked out of the class. The principal would put me in the suspension room or I'd get suspended from school and go home for a couple of days. I just blow up and then get mad at people. They got sick of suspending me and then they expelled me. Then I went to jail and I stopped smoking weed. When I came out from jail I didn't do drugs any more.

Now I'm on house arrest and have to stay in the apartment all the time with my mother. I don't like the way I'm living. I don't want to be on house arrest. I'm going to stay out of trouble in future. If I was off house arrest, that would change the relationship with my mother. You can imagine it would be like this with any household. If you see your son all day, every day, and if you see your mom all day, every day, from the time you wake up, and every night, you're going to get mad and frustrated at one another sometime. That's just like if you're husband and wife.

I don't get along with my mother's boyfriend, Wade. He never works and he just isn't good for my mom. My mom should get back in school or something like that. Maybe she should look for a job, but she needs a good role model in her life, someone to keep her up. That's what me and my brother are trying to tell her all the time, she should get someone better than Wade. He comes here on the weekends, blows all of his money and then tries to blow all of her money on liquor and smokes. My mom needs a man who's going to be a good role model, who's going to do something with his life, so she can take that other step and do it for her life too. I told her I can't make her decisions, no one else can make your decisions, you can only make your own decisions. You're your own person. I told her even if you do pick the decision to stay with Wade, even though it's the wrong decision, you still should still try to do something in your life besides being home. That's why the fights happen.

One time my mom charged me for assault because I pushed her, and she slapped me and punched me, but she called the cops. I went to four different group homes. While I was at the last one I went to anger management. I found it helpful because I didn't have anyone really to talk to there besides the staff, and every week I would go down and talk to a counsellor. He was someone there just to talk to about self-esteem and all my anger problems. He had a crystal ball, and he would tell me to close my eyes, and he would turn it on, and it would make nature noises, and he would say think, think of yourself walking in the woods. It's hard but it would help you right out.

I use that exercise a lot when I get angry. Now the person I talk to most about my problems is my ex-girlfriend. I talk to the child welfare worker too. She calls all the time and she comes by and takes me out for dinner sometimes. I feel comfortable with her and I can tell her anything. She tells me other ways to deal with stuff and she got me into a drug dependency program for a little bit and that was helpful.

I get on with my mother good right now but I wish that she would stop bugging me. Once I flicked the hat off my mom's head and she charged me with assault. It was blown out of proportion. I didn't know what was going on. That's not really an assault. It is technically though. I was mad at her and I just flicked up her hat.

I never hurt her, really hurt her. I may have hurt her with words, but I never made her cry. I've seen her crying over me and my brother though. I know that. So I guess I did hurt her. She worries because she's my legal guardian, and she loves me and she's my mom. I love her too, and I do what she asks me to. Our family life could be better. It's true in the past I pushed my mother. I feel bad about that now and I wouldn't do it again. I watch out for her when her boyfriend's around. He don't treat her badly when I am around. My mother can't take care of herself. Wade was drunk and tried to attack me the other day. He was spitting in my face, pushing me, slapping me, he punched me in my face and then my mom was pushing him away. Then he started hitting on her.

My best memories are when I was little, when I was six. It's okay now, but I could be happier. I want to be a basketball player, or a rapper. I've been playing basketball since I was, like, old enough to pick up a ball. And I love music. I want to get back to school so I can graduate and go to college.

## Karena

I am eighteen. I live by myself. My dad lives with my step-mom and her two kids, who are eight and nine years old. My mom's re-married, and my younger brother and sister live with her in another province. I lived with my mom until I was twelve. She used to beat me all the time. I was the only one that she treated really bad. My dad thinks it's because I am the only one that's his. He thinks that she cheated on him and that my sixteen-year-old brother is not his. My sister is from her husband now. I'm the only kid that she had that was his, and she hates him. Maybe she saw him in me. I was daddy's girl. Mom had really bad problems with my dad, especially when they split up. I always stuck up for him. When my parents got divorced, they were abusive about each other. I fought with my mom over everything, but my dad was the biggest thing we fought about.

We moved around a lot. I never went to the same school two years in a row. I was supposed to graduate last year but I failed twice. I was never really popular. I just wasn't the regular kind of kid from a normal, regular family. Everybody knew my mom was crazy. You can just see the anger in people. You can see that they're not socially attuned. I was one of those kids that got picked on. Once you're one of those kids, you don't make friends easily and so you don't learn social skills. It's like this big vicious cycle. It's terrible and really hard to get out of.

When I told my dad about the beatings he said that I could live with him. I was twelve and I was just a big ball of anger. But that was the first time my dad parented me. He didn't know how to parent me and I didn't know how to be parented. Other people my age had it totally different than I did. I had really strict rules, which was good, now that I look back on it. I wish I had stuck with it and just shut my mouth.

My dad has two boys with his wife. I lived in the basement and everybody else's room was upstairs. I didn't have anything to do. I only had to be responsible for myself and I wasn't used to it. At my mom's, my sister asked for me when she woke up. She was just the best kid. I never, ever had stress with her. She never cried. I was the one that took care of her until I left when she was two. I took care of her more than my mom did. I'd wake up at six in the morning with my mom to help her get my sister ready. Then I'd make the lunches, and make sure that my brother got to school.

My dad is a great guy and when I went to the school near his house, the other kids didn't have a prejudgment of me. I made a lot of friends. I started drinking because that was the thing to do. It was what the kids did every weekend. I was an alcoholic for about two years when I was fifteen, sixteen. It was terrible. I drank every chance I got. Especially when I lived in the group homes. I used to steal and scam people and do anything to get drunk.

At my dad's house I had to be in a couple of hours earlier than everybody else I knew. It was because he knew that I was drinking and smoking and figured if he set my curfews early, I wouldn't have a chance to go out and do it. I kept being late and getting into more trouble. I was really mad at everything because of what happened with my mom, all the abuse, and I didn't listen to anybody. I got into trouble at school, and I got into trouble at home. My dad and I fought all the time. I used to talk to him about my mom and he didn't want to hear it. He told me I needed to go to therapy but I didn't want to. I had been to therapy for almost my whole life. I started going when I was six when my grandfather died because I was really upset about it. I wanted to die too, and I wanted to drop out of school. My mom moved me from one therapist to the next. She was afraid that I would tell them too much.

I moved into a group home and got into more trouble. I was really a bad kid. I fit in at the group home because we all had similar backgrounds. I came from an abusive home and I got in trouble all the time. I thought the world was out to get me. A lot of what I went through was my own fault. But a lot wasn't my fault. I had to deal with all that stuff with my mom. My dad didn't know how to cope with that.

Group homes change your whole life. I remember a girl told me that you can sit here and learn how to steal cars and learn the most fun drug to do, or you can get your education and make it. So group homes can do you good or they can be bad for you, but they definitely are going to change you. I was there four years. Now I'm on assistance and I have my own apartment. I've spent a lot of time working on what my mother did to me. I hope that I never do anything like that. I can't hold it against her. Just because they're your mom or your dad, doesn't mean that they have to be perfect.

I didn't talk to my mom for about two and a half years. When I got kicked out of my dad's house for the second time, I called my mom and told her about the alcohol and stuff. We started talking from then. She told me that I had to stop drinking and get my life together. She gave me inspiration. I couldn't stand my dad being disappointed in me, so I wasn't going to tell him that I was doing really shitty stuff. He thought of it like experimenting, like it's a normal teenage thing to do. But it was a lot more than that and he didn't know. My mom knew because I didn't really care what she thought. She just convinced me to at least slow down on it, to get my school marks up a bit. She told me that I'm smart enough to do it and that she didn't want to see me throw my life away.

When I got kicked out of my dad's, we had a bad fight. I can't remember what we were arguing about. Something about school I think. He picked me up and threw me out on the deck and I had a bloody nose. When I saw my own blood I came back. I just started whaling on him, and I don't remember how bad or for how long, but I remember he showed me later on that day that his whole chest was green with bruises. It was terrible. I felt so bad. I still feel bad about that. It was years ago. I was an aggressive and violent person, and my dad didn't know how to deal with me. He told me before that if it was just him then he would have me home, but he couldn't have me living with his wife and her two kids too. Then it's a different story.

At one point I ended up living with my cousin and she tried to kill me. She's manic-depressive and was doing street and prescription drugs, and she went crazy. My dad came and put me in a shelter for a couple of weeks. Then I lived with his friend, then with a family for about a year. Then I moved back into group homes because I missed it. When I was with somebody else's family it worked really well but it made me kind of upset. It made me wonder how come it works with their family, but not with my own. I was a whole lot more mature, easier to get along with, and wasn't crazy anymore, but eventually I realized that I didn't like living in the group homes anymore either. That's when I got my own place.

I'm trying to get through school. I don't really want to have my own kids because I can't be sure that I can give them the best. People mess up, and I'd be afraid I'd screw up on a kid. There are a lot of things that I wish I had done differently, but then I realize that if I had done them differently I wouldn't be where I am today. I wouldn't have learned as much, I wouldn't have made the friends that I have made, and I wouldn't have had the opportunity that I have now.

## Crystal

Today I had a police officer talk to me at school. I threatened another girl by telling her that I am going to kill her. This girl angered me. She spread rumours about me. She said that I was taking drugs and drinking at a party on the weekend. I had to let her know that I was not happy. I made these threats at school. I was called in and the police officer explained to me that I could go to jail for uttering death threats. So anybody that utters death threats can go to jail. That is really serious.

I live with my sister, my mother and my stepfather. I do sometimes react badly, and I'm verbally bad towards Mommy and Daddy. My mommy says that I am physically abusive but I can't remember it. Most of the arguments start because of stupid things. The stupidest things you will not believe it. The other day I went shopping with my mommy. She said I could have certain clothes but not too much. I tried to push her to buy more. I know it is bad but I just tried.

My sister, Gabriella, and I have a lot of fights. We had one today in the car. My sister did not want to let me speak. Mommy said to ignore her but Gabriella screamed at me. The fight was over whose turn it was to sit in front. I just ignored her and went on talking to Mommy. I don't get angry anymore. You can try and call me names — I just walk away.

I share everything with my best friend. We've been friends for years. I have a lot of friends. I get along with most people. People think I am funny. I like doing really special work for school in projects. I hate it when you look at a project and it looks like it was put together in five minutes. My teacher said my art project was the best in the class the other day.

When we were in Ontario before Mommy and Daddy met, Mommy had a boyfriend Alex. This boyfriend was horrible to us. I use to hide in a secret place. There was a false door where you could go into and he did not know about this. It drove him wild when he was looking for us. One night he saw the light shining underneath the opening. I was really afraid of him. Things are better since we have moved. This is a nicer house than our other one. In our house Daddy is stricter than Mommy. He makes all the rules. Daddy used to get physical with me. He pushed me into the room, but he is not allowed to touch me anymore.

When Mommy left for the shelter just before Christmas I was really afraid. We said bad things and everyone was angry. Mommy came back the following day. We all stopped fighting that evening. I think it was a good thing Mommy left because we stopped fighting. I thought she'd leave us for good. It was the second time we were alone without Mommy. After we arrived here from Ontario, Mommy became ill and had to stay in the hospital. Daddy couldn't look after us so we went to live with my uncle and aunt. It was horrible. They would give all the best stuff to their children and all the horrible stuff to us. They would buy their children Nike's and we would get hand-me-downs. My biggest fear is that my Mommy will leave me and never come back. That is why you should never leave without saying goodbye because you never know what can happen to you.

## Conclusion

We are grateful to the teens who told us the story from their point of view and admire their honesty. These teens, like the mothers, were all very different. They came from different social classes and different cultures, had different experiences and different ways of looking at the abuse. As with the mothers, after their stories were written, we invited the teens to change anything they didn't agree with, including the pen name we had given them. The only change requested was in one pen name. We chose three of the stories to include in this book. Karena is now on her own. Older and wiser, she is trying to put her life in order. Crystal still lives with her family and continues to be abusive. We have had no further contact with Jordan.

At times, during the interview, Jordan was a delightful, sweet person. He also showed considerable anger. At his mother's request, Annemarie and I interviewed Jordan and Deborah in their home — a small apartment. Jordan sat in the living room watching television while we listened to Deborah. He could hear what she was saying and interrupted the interview with increasing verbal aggression. To stop the disruption, I went into the living room and sat beside Jordan on the couch. He was extremely agitated and for a few minutes, I thought he would hit me. I gently explained that it was important for his mother to tell her story and he would have the opportunity to give his story later. The atmosphere was tense and threatening, but eventually he calmed and agreed to remain quiet. When his turn to talk to us came, Jordan told us he had attended anger management classes, and they had helped a great deal. The anger we saw suggested he did not have a very realistic self-assessment. Neither did Crystal. Her declaration that she no longer gets angry was not borne out in the behaviour I witnessed in her home; it was no less threatening than Jordan's. Teens also have selective memories, or perhaps they chose not to disclose some details. Crystal, for example, omitted to tell us that on the way home from the shopping trip, she spat on her mother, who was trying to drive. Karena was more reflexive and displayed no aggression, but she did describe her younger self as "just a big ball of anger."

Teenagers are typically self-absorbed and slow to take responsibility for their behaviour, and our interviews showed that abusive teens are no less so than most other teens. While they regretted what happened, they focused on themselves, and even when they thought they understood what was going on, they felt that circumstances or other people were equally responsible for the teens' actions. Rather than perceiving the problem to be his behaviour, Jordan saw it as a problem with his "relationship with his mother" and believed that would change if he weren't under house arrest. Crystal didn't focus on her behaviour as the root of the problem either. Her description of what happened when she threatened one of her schoolmates revealed that she believes she shouldn't hurt others, not because her behaviour is wrong, but because of what might happen to her as a consequence. Of the three teens, Karena took the most responsibility for her actions. She admitted she was "a bad kid" and saw that much was her own fault, but she doesn't say, "In spite of my background, my behaviour was unacceptable." In fact, she also believes that her behaviour was the result of her parents' inability to parent and having come from an abusive home.

Not being adequately parented was a theme that emerged in the interviews. Karena said her father didn't know how to parent. It is interesting that, even though the relationship with her mother was disastrous, when she was living with her mother and caring for her little sister, packing lunches and making sure her brothers got to school, Karena was happier than when she stayed with her father and didn't have any responsibilities. Jordan felt that his mother couldn't take care of herself and he had to take a parental role with her. Although he insisted that he "can't make her decisions," he said he watched out for her when her boyfriend was around. He criticized his mother for not doing "anything with her life." This closely echoes what parents say to their children, not the reverse.

Instability and violence in the family were also key factors in their lives. Karena said her family "moved around a lot" and she didn't go to the same school two years in a row. Her times with her mother, then her father, were extremely explosive and she clearly suffered from their abuse of each other. She also lived with a cousin who was mentally unstable and threatening, and in a group home where violence and delinquency were common. It was when she was in the stable environment of the family friend that she behaved well, although she was envious of their family life compared with her own. Crystal's family moved and changed numerous times, and she and her sister were exposed to the violence of their father and both of their mother's subsequent partners, who were abusive to the girls. It is interesting that Crystal abuses her mother, even though she was full of dread that her mother would leave her, and felt "you never know what can happen to you." Jordan's family also moved numerous times and faced the instability of poverty more than once.

The teens did not think through, or really understand, the impact of their behaviour on their parents. They minimized the abuse with statements like:

> *It was blown out of proportion.*
> *We said bad things and everyone was angry.*
> *I didn't know what was going on.*
> *That's not really an assault.*
> *I was mad at her and I just flicked up her hat.*

Jordan stated that he may have hurt his mother with words, but had never made her cry. It took a moment's reflection for him to realize that this was not true, that he had seen her crying over him, and that he had hurt her. In an equally unthoughtful statement he said that he was obedient to his mother. This was clearly false. Crystal too didn't have a realistic understanding of herself.

Their peers also played a role in the behaviour of Karena, Jordan and Crystal. It was because of peer pressure, the desire to be liked and not to be picked on, that Karena began drinking, and it was in the group home that she learned other delinquent behaviours; Jordan talked of conflict with his mother over his behaviour when he was with friends, and Crystal spoke of fights with other girls.

They all swear that they will not continue to abuse. Unfortunately, we have only been able to follow up with Crystal's family to find out what has happened since we talked to them, but in that family, the abuse has not stopped. In fact it has worsened.

# 6. Who Is Doing the Abusing?

*You look at your family, and they are the people you know will always be there, so sometimes you spill your guts and it might not always come out the way you want it to sound. (Lana, age seventeen)*

We have heard the stories of three teens, Karena, Jordan and Crystal. This chapter discusses what mothers told us about their teens and looks at what researchers and writers say on the topic. When conducting my research, as I had with the mothers who were being abused, I tried to establish the individual characteristics common to teens who abuse. I looked at whether boys are more likely to abuse than girls, and at the age and size of the teens; I explored the connection between the teens' exposure to adult violence and the ways children learn to be aggressive. I also attempted to find out if there were any patterns of school behaviour or peer influence, or if teens who abuse are more or less likely to use alcohol or drugs, or have a mental disability. Finally, I asked the mothers if their teens felt guilty and showed remorse.

## Gender

"What kind of teen would hit his mother?" people ask, usually assuming the teen is male. In 1997 a web newspaper, *The Sacramento Bee*, carried an article called "Abuse of parents by teens increases: Victims frequently silenced by shame," in which the author assumes that it is only boys who commit parent abuse. While there is evidence that more boys than girls are violent towards their parents (Charles 1986; Evans and Warren-Sohlberg 1988; Gallagher 2004; Harbin and Madden 1979), it often comes as a surprise that girls also abuse their parents and can be as physically violent as boys. Researchers who find that more physical violence against parents is committed by adolescent boys than girls state that the difference is only slight (Agnew and Huguley 1989; Artz 1998; Charles 1986; Cornell and Gelles 1982; Evans and Warren-Sohlberg 1988; Kumagai 1981; Paulson et al. 1990). Dr. Xavier Plaus, Director of the Roberts/Smart Residential Treatment Centre in Ottawa, who has had many years' experience working with some of Canada's most violent children, says the Centre houses as many girls as boys (personal communication 2003). The evidence is clearly contradictory. I suspect that boys continue to be more violent than girls, but girls are more violent than they have been in the past. We do know that the majority of violent crimes are committed by men and that men are socialized to be more aggressive, dominant and competitive than women.

## Age and Size

There are differences of opinion about the age of the children when the abuse starts. Service providers interviewed in my 1995 parent abuse study said they believe that the foundation of abusive behaviour begins long before the children are teenagers. Most of the parents said the abuse began when the child was between twelve and sixteen, although some did see signs of violent behaviour at earlier ages. Theresa was one mother who said that looking back she can see a pattern that started when her son was a small child. At the age of two David would pinch, bite and use his toys as weapons to get his own way. Connie's daughter was also a difficult baby, and by the time she was in school, her behaviour was a problem, "It was like that right from the start. The rules are for everybody else, not her." In the early years, however, the parents see the behaviour as a "tantrum" rather than as abuse or as a sign of things to come. Most parents have experienced a screaming, demanding three-year-old in the grocery store, for instance, but would think of it as typical behaviour for that age group, an aggressive stage that the child will outgrow. Dr. Plaus believes that many of the boys at his centre have stayed in the "terrible two" stage, whereas girls generally don't begin to be violent until puberty.

As they get bigger, teenagers' greater physical size may make them more threatening, and parents then begin to identify the child's behaviour as abusive (Agnew and Huguley 1989; Charles 1986; Harbin and Madden 1979; Kumagai 1981; Paulson et al. 1990). In Canada, young people are maturing physically at a younger age than ever before in history, a trend attributed to our improved understanding of nutrition and our improved access to nutritional food. Some people believe that the bigger and stronger the teens are, the more violent they are towards their parents. However, it has been suggested that the level of physical force used against parents is inversely related to the teen's size and strength, i.e., stronger teens tend to use intimidation and control tactics against parents, while smaller and less powerful teens use physical force (Harbin and Madden 1979; Warren 1978).

There is no agreement among researchers about which specific age groups are more abusive. According to Agnew and Huguley: "Cornell and Gelles (1982) found that age was unrelated to parent assault, although when results were examined separately by sex, they found that the rate of severe assault increased as boys aged and decreased as girls aged" (1989: 701). Paulson et al. who interviewed 445 youths and an equal number of parents, found that, "Younger offspring were less physically assaultive towards their parents. Only 7% of the youngest group (ages 9–11) hit one or both parents contrasting with 17% of the 12–14-year olds, and 16% of those 15–17 years of age" (1990: 125). Peek et al. found that although there was an increase in "father-oriented violence as the youth in our sample grow older, the level of overall violence toward their parents (i.e., "hit either parent") seems to drop — most noticeably between their sophomore and junior years.... Perhaps the safest conclusion is that male youths' overall violence toward parents does not increase during the ages in which their skills in the use of violence probably do increase" (1985: 1055). Assault declined with age among the boys in their sample, and Paulson et al. (1990) reports that in their research, "younger offspring were less physically assaultive towards their parents" (1990: 125). According to Eckstein, "Researchers do agree more conflict is evident between parents and adolescents in the early adolescence period than in the middle adolescence, more adolescent-parent conflict in middle than in late adolescences, and more conflict in early adolescence than in late adolescence (Comstock 1994; Kinloch 1985). Though the frequency of conflict episodes seems to decline between adolescents and parents in middle and late age adolescents, negative affects towards the parent by the adolescent increases during these conflict episodes. To summarize, adolescent-parent conflict is less frequent but more heated in middle adolescence than in early adolescence" (2002: 48).

## Family Violence

One of the reasons people think boys are more likely to be physically violent than girls is that, in Canadian society, men are more violent than women. It is predictable, therefore, that boys, more than girls, will identify with their fathers and copy their behaviour (Bandura 1973; Cornell and Gelles 1982). As we saw in Chapter Two, an astounding number of children are exposed to violence in their families. Studies in the United States put the number at between three and ten million children every year and state that almost a quarter of teens who abuse their mothers had fathers who had battered their wives (Graham-Bermann 1998; Jaffe et al. 1990; Kerig 1999; Sudermann and Jaffe 1999). While it is important to remember that many abusive teens have not been exposed to family violence, studies show that teenagers who are violent are more likely to have witnessed abuse than non-violent teens.

We know that being exposed to violence can have a negative impact on children, whether they actually witness the abuse or not. When they grow up seeing their mother victimized, they may treat her in the same abusive way (Dauvergne and Johnson 2001; Edleson 1999; Hughes 1989; Jaffe et al. 1990; Kerig 1999; Maker et al. 1998). In families where the children are also abused, there is evidence that teens' violence is caused by "a combination of parental aggression, inadequate discipline and negative attitudes towards the child" (Shulman and Seiffge-Krenke 1997: 181).

Girls sometimes resent their mothers for subjecting themselves and their children to the violence of their husband or partner, and for being submissive and depressed. This rage may not be expressed until the child reaches adolescence, when, angry at their mothers for "failing to pro-tect" themselves and their families, they idealize the abuser and model their behaviour on their fathers'. One woman said her daughter would screen her phone calls and she wouldn't find out till a few days later that people had called. Then added, "Her father used to do that." Pauline said her son yells at her, calls her names, puts her down, threatens to put her head through the wall or to throw her out of the window, "like his father did." Pauline believes her husband's abuse affected her family, and that is why her teens abuse her now.

## Learned Aggression

Teens act out in their families what they learn from society: that is, women are not as strong or powerful as men. Sibylle Artz discusses this issue in her book, *Sex, Power and the Violent School Girl*. Artz believes that the girls she studied saw few positives in being female:

> A girl has to be vigilant about staying thin; she is restricted with regard to the kinds of activities she can undertake; she is less

respected and less important than a boy. She is routinely subjected to sexual discrimination and harassment. If she attempts to take the initiative or experiment sexually, she is a "slut" and deserves a beating. If a woman has children, she faces a great deal of pain, and if her husband is present to see the "mess," she risks losing him because, through pregnancy and childbirth, her body becomes unattractive. (1998: 177)

It may be thought that young women today are rebelling against this concept of girls and women, but researchers state that the opposite is true: girls do not recognize the value or power of females and believe that females are inferior to males and the only way they can attain power is by attracting dominant males (Totten 2003). Artz states that girls learn that "men are far more important and more powerful than women, and that men's importance is not connected to the contributions they make to the greater good. Rather, it is bound up in their being stronger and more forceful than women."

Young women see that, as the victims of ongoing violence and denigration, women lack confidence in themselves as human beings and as parents. This leads to self-blaming and makes them vulnerable, and it is usually vulnerable people who are abused. Being submissive, a strategy women use to cope with abuse, can lead to further victimization. These girls want to be as powerful as males and are angry that they are not. They see that their mothers are not either. They attempt to attach themselves to success by imitating the aggressive behaviour of males rather than identifying with the "weakness" of women. Even though their anger is sometimes inappropriately expressed, it can be understood.

The sad thing is, as part of a tragic re-enactment, when they grow up in homes where women are not as valued as men and power takes the form of abuse, children learn that abuse is acceptable. If it has been occurring for years or generations, abusive behaviour is considered normal, as this woman confirmed:

*My ex-husband was abusive to me, in every way except physical — emotionally, verbally, constantly putting me down. So, I guess that I had fourteen years of training to be abused by my children. I lived in a small town at that time and compared to the other women in the community my relationship with my husband was pretty good — at least he didn't hit me.*

Growing up with violence gives teens the message that violence can be an appropriate way to behave and to get what they want. Mark Totten believes that children are not born violent, they learn to be violent by seeing it around them, within the family, in society, on television (see also Totten 2003; Pipher 1994). Teens who are the victims of physical, sexual or emotional abuse, sometimes by their fathers or stepfathers, may abuse in an effort to protect themselves or a younger sibling (Brezina 1999; Browne and Hamilton 1998; Wells 1987). The abuse they perpetrate expresses their anger, and it is occasionally directed at the offending parent. Unfortunately, they often focus their retaliation on their non-abusive parent, usually the mother. This may be an attempt to "tell" her about the abuse that was occurring or to express intense anger and resentment for not having been protected, or it may be an expression of society's tendency to blame mothers when others abuse their children.

Children who are raised in emotionally abusive environments often internalize a negative perception of themselves. They commonly feel vulnerable and isolated and have low self-esteem and difficulty feeling close or "attached" to their parents. Some use abusive behaviour as an expression of anger toward parents or as a desperate attempt to gain attention or create an emotional connection with them. According to the Canadian Centre for Justice Statistics, "Children who are exposed to adults or teenagers physically fighting in the home were more likely to exhibit physical aggression, emotional disorders, hyperactivity, and to commit delinquent acts against property" (Dauvergne and Johnson 2001).

Although family violence is pervasive in homes where there is parent abuse, not all children who have been exposed to family violence become aggressive. We do not really know why people, including children, react differently to their experiences. Some people seem to live through harrowing traumas and grow up to be well-balanced, loving and respectful. Others are damaged by the experience. It is much the same with children of alcoholics. Some become alcoholics, others do not. We don't know if the violent behaviour is actually caused by the experiences but it does seem to be associated. Often, when we hear a teen's history, when we know what they have seen and heard and experienced, we think, "No wonder they behave badly!" When we reflect on the terrifying influence of violence in children's lives, particularly when they have been exposed to their mothers being beaten, it seems plausible that the tendency towards violence will emerge later (Sudermann and Jaffe 1999). Both Totten and Plaus believe that if children who experience or are exposed to violence get support from family, friends, school or somewhere else, they can grow up to be neither perpetrators nor victims of violence.

After they have removed themselves and their children from an abusive relationship, some mothers find a gentler, more caring partner. However, many abusive, controlling teens, like Theresa's son, David, refuse to accept this. There is evidence that the presence of a second adult is a deterrent to violence, and children who grow up in families where there is only one adult are more likely to be abusive (Dornbusch 1985: 185). However, other scholars find that parent abuse is more likely in what they call "intact" families (Agnew and Huguley 1989; Charles 1986).

There is also evidence that children who were hit by their parents are more likely to abuse than children who were not (Brezina 1999). The same is true for children who have been the victims of severe physical or sexual abuse by a parent or another adult within their nuclear or extended family, or outside the family altogether (Agnew 1992; Agnew and Huguley 1989; Brezina 1999; Browne and Hamilton 1998; Carlson 1990; Cornell and Gelles 1982; Evans and Warren-Sohlberg 1988; Kratcoski 1982; Libon 1989; Livingston 1986; Patterson 1980; Peek et al. 1985; Wells 1987). Dr. Plaus says that more than half of the girls who are residing at his centre have been sexually abused. Children who have been the victims of violence sometimes suffer from mental health problems like depression and low self-esteem. Many are aggressive and violent. Drug and alcohol abuse is common, although not necessarily any more common than in children who have not been the victims of violence. As a rule, boys and girls respond differently: boys usually become violent themselves, whereas girls often become the victims of abuse in their own adult relationships. Sadly, many children who have been abused believe they are responsible for the abuse. If they do not get help to deal with this "guilt," they internalize it and often act out aggressively. Similarly, teens who were raised in emotionally abusive environments have very low self-esteem. In a way, they act out being the person they are accused of being: a person not worthy of love or attention, and one who is stupid and no good. These teens feel vulnerable and isolated.

## School and Peers

Another area in which there are no identifiable common patterns is the teens' school achievement. Many mothers have told me their children are doing well in school, "on the principal's list," "on the honour list," "high achievers" and "making top marks." In the 1995 study, only one-third of the mothers said that the children had academic difficulties. Other parents believe their children are not performing as well as they could at school, not because they can't do the work, but because they skip classes. One academic study found that abusive teens are more likely to be bored at school than non-abusive teens (Paulson et al. 1990), and another found that teens who are suspended from school are more likely to abuse their parents, possibly as a result of the conflict over the suspension (Eckstein 2002).

As with academic achievement, some abusive teens get along well socially at school and with their friends. Mothers said things like: "He's quite well liked. He can be charming, funny, and he can be nice to be around," and "Some people find it hard to believe that he acts the way he does to me. He'd never talk back to my friend. When he stayed with her he helped with the dishes, watched the kids, was perfectly behaved." But slightly more than half of the teens in the 1995 study did have social problems with peers or teachers at school.

Teens can feel under a great deal of pressure at school and from their peers and experience the school environment as violent, unsafe and disrespectful. Karena told us she was picked on at school, and once she was identified as "one of those kids," she couldn't make friends. Teens experience violence and are threatened by the other students. Some retaliate.

Children learn from others at school that being violent is an effective strategy to gain power and control. One young woman said:

*School is really violent and abusive. You should hear the way the kids talk, they say, "Don't mess with me," and they mean it. My friend was walking along one day and some guy comes up to him and says, "Where's that $20 you owe me?" If you're half-ways nervous, if you're not a cool person, you'd have to get the money for him even if you never borrowed it, otherwise you live in fear of being beaten up.*

Children who do not do well academically sometimes learn negative behaviour at school. These children are often labelled as "slow," "stupid" or "difficult," and they internalize this. If they get recognition as a result of bad behaviour, they continue with such behaviours. Another way they attempt to get a sense of control over the ways in which they are defined is to be "bad." This involves taking drugs, drinking alcohol and getting involved in crime or violence. Inevitably, this creates family conflict, which increases the likelihood of violence.

Teens quickly learn that if they are not accepted, they may become the object of scorn and bullying. Dr. Plaus believes that a high percentage of youth who are extremely violent were the victims of bullying at school, as young as six and seven. There is evidence that many of the young boys who are responsible for terrible shootings at their schools, like the two at Columbine High School in Colorado and the fourteen-year-old who shot two students at Myles High School in Taber, Alberta, in 1999, were the victims of bullying. Although recently schools have made huge strides in dealing with bullying, children continue to be victimized. There are few outlets for adolescents to deal with the stress they experience at school, and if they don't drop out of school, they often displace their rage and act out with violent and abusive actions where it is safe for them to do so, and that is usually at home. Coming home from school upset, they try to feel more in control by taking out their anger on their parents.

They also choose friends who display violent behaviours in the home. Theresa's son chose "rough" friends early, and when he started school his friends were always the troubled toughies. It is natural that, as they become teenagers, children start to pull away from their parents and gain more independence. Unfortunately, this is the time when they are perhaps their most emotionally unstable and insecure, and if they have a stable adult in their lives, they pull away from the one person they can trust. Teenagers are, as Cornel West, an American theologian and author of two books on teens (Hewlett and West 1998; West 1993), puts it, "hungry for identity, meaning and self-worth," but the friends they turn to for support are usually equally insecure and not always the best influence. This alone is cause for conflict in many families. In an effort to keep control, parents want their children to communicate and be open with them, but the teens are sharing their closest secrets, not with their parents, but with their friends. In the face of peer pressure, which is extremely strong during the teenage years, teenagers usually lack the maturity to exercise self-control, and this can lead to other forms of destructive behaviour.

These teens need adult guidance and leadership. It was when Karena moved to another school and finally began to make friends that she began drinking because "that was the thing to do. It was what the kids did every weekend." Karena was an alcoholic by the time she fifteen. One teen told me she is "really influenced" by her friends. She said, "You see one of your friends being disrespectful and you kind of copy them." Another said, "I was pissed off because I was born so I took it out on my parents." In her opinion, teens are confused but don't know how to express it. They feel powerless because everyone is telling them what to do at a time when they want to be controlling others. She believes that, "If you see your friends abusing and getting away with it, you might want to try it." Teenagers are often not afraid to abuse their mothers in front of their friends. In Chapter Two we heard from a mother who said her daughter screamed abuse at her in front of the girl's friends and from another who said that her daughter threatened to ask a friend to break the mother's knees. We also heard in Chapter Two that teens in conflict with their friends bring this tension home and take it out on their mothers.

When people are abusive they like to have the support of other people. They justify their actions by thinking that others agree with them. It is not uncommon for men who abuse their wives, for instance, to tell sexist jokes or make comments at work like, "We all know women need to be kept under control, right?" A woman told me that in the staff room at work, a co-worker casually mentioned he'd hit his wife the previous night. No one responded. Perhaps they were too shocked or embarrassed, but the silence could easily have been taken as affirmation: it wasn't a big enough deal for his co-workers to say anything. Teens are no different in wanting complicity. They may be under even more pressure than adults to be popular with their peers, and they like to think their friends side with them.

Teens are under a great deal of pressure to be accepted by their peers. They quickly learn that to be accepted, they have to be "cool." "Cool" is defined, not by the teens themselves, but is manufactured by advertising agencies that bombard them with seductive ads for all the material goods they "must" have. But teens do not usually have the economic means to access these material goods for themselves, and instead they pressure their parents, sometimes abusively, for them. Teens from wealthy families may be so used to getting everything they want that they abuse if their parents finally say no (Gallagher 2004). Ads directed at young people compel them to present themselves in an inappropriate sexualized way, and many teens feel they must emulate scantily clad young pop stars in order to fit in. To be cool is to have "attitude," which means adopting a rude and hostile stance. It is difficult for a teenager to opt not to be cool. They feel they have to be in control to avoid being victimized and to learn not to show weakness in front of their peers. Many teens find this peer pressure intolerable. Their fragile self-confidence shatters and they feel vulnerable, alone and alienated from everyone and become depressed and withdrawn. Others act abusively. In an attempt to survive, rather than connect with their parents or another authority figure, they try to form close friendships with other teens. Some join gangs. A number of the boys Mark Totten (2003) wrote about abandoned their families and sought a sense of belonging, status and acceptance with their friends. Some of these boys abused to impress their friends, and others were recruited into gangs.

## Substance Use and Abuse

Socially deviant activities such as drug and alcohol use and criminal activities, including shoplifting, fraud, break and enter, theft, violent crime and/or prostitution, are common among abusive teens. More than half of the parents we interviewed suspected or knew that their teen was using drugs or alcohol. However, it is unlikely that teens who abuse their parents misuse alcohol and drugs more than teens who are not abusive. According to Health Canada, about a quarter of our teens have tried marijuana, and this number has slowly increased since the 1980s (Health Canada 1999). Adolescence is the time when people are curious about things they've never done and are most likely to experiment. Experimenting is not necessarily a problem, but Health Canada concludes that children who use marijuana are also more likely to use alcohol and smoke cigarettes. They are also more likely to spend time with other teens who engage in the same behaviour and are more likely to feel pressured at school, skip classes and bully others. However, no causal relationship has been established, so we do not know if this is anything more than coincidence.

Although substance abuse does not cause violent behaviour, parents report that when their teen is using drugs, the parents sometimes notice a sudden, drastic change in the child's behaviour. They become more moody, anxious, depressed and sometimes more violent, and their school performance and peer relationships change. Drug use may lower the teens' inhibitions and they may do things that they would not do otherwise. When they are using drugs, teens may show no sense of remorse. As one mother said, "Her anger was much worse when she was on drugs. There was a cutting edge to her. There was no feeling. The drugs wiped out all her feelings."

Sometimes it is the parents who are abusing drugs or alcohol, and their teens may feel abandoned and be angry with them for being unavailable and emotionally absent. Threatening to reveal their parents' substance abuse is one method teens use to try to control their parents. Some teens whose parents are alcohol and substance abusers may, as psychologist Mary Pipher says, connect love with "anger, violence, unpredictability and shame" (1994: 192). Pauline has been drug-free for the past two years and is now ashamed to admit that when she and her husband were taking hard drugs, they stole and sold their children's belongings to buy crack cocaine. Her teens are very abusive to her now.

## Mental Disabilities

In my 1995 study, nearly half of the parents said that their children had been clinically diagnosed with attention-deficit/hyperactivity disorder (ADHD or ADD), oppositional defiant disorder or conduct disorders, including adolescent adjustment disorder, reactive attachment disorder, oppositional defiant disorder; disruptive behaviour disorder and learning disorders, and three of the teens were diagnosed with a biochemical mental disorder, such as schizophrenia, bipolar disorder or autism.

A number of parents whose teens had not been diagnosed believed their teen had a mental, emotional or learning disability or suffered from fetal alcohol syndrome, as the teens had problems with affect regulation, impulse control, social empathy and interpersonal skills. After the diagnosis, prescribed drugs can help to control the teen's violent behaviour and help the teen see their behaviour more clearly. However, some teens abuse the drugs they are prescribed. Other teens, like Karena, are the children of parents with unstable mental health. In these situations, youth may assume a caretaker role and that can lead to feelings of resentment toward parents.

## Guilt and Remorse

Perhaps of greatest importance in understanding parent abuse is teenagers' own misconceptions of their behaviour. Teens rarely defined their behaviour as abusive, but rather say they had "a fight" with their parents. They also seldom appear to take responsibility for their behaviour, as this mother said of her son: "There was no remorse, he felt totally justified in his behaviour. He was resentful of others objecting to his behaviour." It is typical to hear a distressed parent say, "There's no guilt, nothing, no concern at all. She walks out of the house without even saying goodbye." Some parents shake their heads in disbelief that after many years, when the children have moved into adulthood, they still do not recognize that their behaviour was abusive. Theresa said that David, who is now in his twenties, still seems unaffected by any of the stress and pain he caused her in the past. Counsellors, police and researchers find a similar reaction from many of the men they work with who abuse their partners (Harbin and Madden 1979). These men usually believe that their victims are responsible for the violence, or they minimize the abuse. Deborah's son, Jordan, did this when he said, "I didn't really hurt her," but he is one of the few who admits he was abusive, and, at least when he talked to me, seemed to be remorseful.

Teens are notoriously self-focused, and it is clear that they seldom understand how much pain they are inflicting, but some teens are fully aware. Perhaps they show no signs of remorse or guilt, not because they don't feel it, but because being ashamed and guilty for what they've done can makes them feel very vulnerable. Instead of admitting their vulnerability, they try to make themselves feel more powerful by showing intense anger toward their parents. They may be filled with self-hatred for what they have done, and that can be destructive too. The pattern of the abuse can be similar to that of wife/partner assault where some perpetrators go through a "honeymoon period" (Walker 1983) in which they say they hate themselves for what they have done and promise to improve their behaviour and never to re-abuse. But it seldom lasts. Irene's son went to live with his sister for a while, then he returned home full of remorse and would hug his mother and talk about what he had done. But Irene said that he was soon involved with his friends and assaulting her again.

## Conclusion

Teens who abuse their parents come from both socially advantaged and disadvantaged families; they may be parented by people who are too authoritarian, overly-permissive or absent; some have experienced abuse or have seen their mothers abused, others have not. In other words, teens who abuse come from a wide variety of families. What they seem to have in common is that they abuse to get their own way and are attempting to control their parents. "You can't make me. I can make my own decisions!" they say. They know their parents' soft spots and aim where it will hurt. Another commonality is that, like men who abuse their intimate partners, the teens vent their anger, whatever its source, on their parents. Teens also seldom name or take responsibility for their behaviour, perhaps because by not naming it, they feel there is no problem.

There are patterns, including substance abuse, abusive peer groups, problems at school and mental ill health. However, there are many exceptions. It is clear that not all youth who use drugs, have abusive peers and problems at school or are mentally ill abuse their parents, and not all teens who abuse their parents fit into any of those categories.

# 7. The Final Blow

## Clare

With lights flashing, the squad car sped into our yard. The impact of calling 911 was soon to unfold. The counsellor our son had been seeing told us, "You need to call the police next time it happens. I am afraid he is going to harm you."

I cannot remember what insignificant event precipitated Matthew's behaviour. It could have been anything. Maybe I didn't do a load of laundry he wanted that day. It's like living with a tornado. You never know when or why the destruction will come, or what will happen.

I heard the knife drawer open in the kitchen, and I heard Kris saying, "No Matthew!" I rushed to put myself between my two children, never really believing he would harm his sister. He loves her. In fact, he loves us all. So why is he doing this? I grabbed Kris and our other son, Martin, and headed to the car. For the moment we were safe. In desperation I called my husband for help. I knew David wouldn't back away. He was determined to save us all, including his first-born son. Matthew came out of the house swinging a baseball bat. He smashed the siding on the house. He smashed doors and walls.

When the police arrived we all went back into the house. This was his first encounter with the police. He had idolized the police when he was little. He had wanted to be a policeman when he grew up. When they jumped out of their cars, hands ready to pull their guns, Matthew dropped the baseball bat. They handcuffed him. How can anyone imagine the incredible pain I felt as I watched my child, in whom I'd seen such talent, such potential, being led away in handcuffs, driven away in a police car? A piece of me died right there.

The following day at the police station, we watched as Matthew was led into a room to meet with us and one of the arresting officers. He had been held overnight in a cell. Lights left on, no blanket. This was his first offence, and they were determined to scare him straight. The officer warned, "If we are called again and you have a weapon, a bat or anything else, we will shoot you. And if your parents get in the way, we'll shoot them too."

There was a next time, but we didn't call the police right away. It was Christmas night. Another nightmare. Another story.

## Mary

I opened my jewellery basket and saw the old box which held my great grandfather's watch. I touched the velvet — smooth and cool. I remembered the feel of the watch — the grooved winder, the sound of clicking open the watch cover, the silence of the watch — it hadn't worked for decades. The watch connects me with my family, generations of family who had worn the watch and then the generations who had stored the watch for its sentimental value. The engraving said, "To E.M. from D.M. with love, 1843" — love that had passed through those many generations.

I opened the velvet box with these memories, wanting to hold the watch again, to feel the connection with my family. My stomach dropped, my mouth went dry. There was no watch. Only the velvet ring that had held the watch. There was no contrast between the gold of the watch against the blue velvet. I could not rub my fingers over the engraving. There was no watch.

This was the final blow — and there had been blows — physical blows, emotional blows, financial blows. Memories of slaps came back, the kicks, the swearing, the continual put downs, the continually disappearing money. Year after year.

I asked my daughter about the watch. "It's just an old watch! You never use it. It just sits in the jewellery basket. You never give me the money I deserve, so I sold it. Who cares about an old watch anyway?"

That was it. The final blow. I don't need to put up with this behaviour any more. "You'll have to move. I don't deserve this."

The power of those words, "It was only an old watch," gave me the strength to make the changes I needed.

# 8. Looking for Causes

*I questioned myself till I drove myself crazy.*

Everyone seems to have an opinion about why children behave abusively, and frequently their opinion is that the children aren't being parented properly. Even parents think they must have done something wrong and beat themselves up with anxiety searching for what it may have been. Although I discuss possible causes of parent abuse in this chapter, I need to begin with a caution. Too often service providers get mired down looking for causes and miss the first, essential priority: to help parents stop the abuse and regain their leadership in the family. It is worth repeating that none of us is a perfect parent, and blaming the parents is not just an inadequate explanation, it is often just plain wrong. Only when the abuse has stopped and parents are once again in loving and compassionate control of their children, should people look for causes, if they think it will be helpful.

Looking for causes is not a good place to start, whatever mistakes were made, because seldom is there just one identifiable reason why the abuse is happening and seldom can we find a simple answer or a clear cause. A myriad of causes is possible; societal and cultural values, family dynamics and the individual development of the child may all play a role. These dynamics are "nested": every individual is situated within a family that is situated within a social culture. The social culture affects and influences the family, which in turn affects and influences the individual, and each individual has their own characteristics and personality. The family may be the primary influence on a child's life, but families operate in a social framework, and children are also influenced by their gender, race, class, ability and religion. Sometimes these dynamics are so related or intertwined it is almost impossible to separate them and to figure out what is a cause and what is a result of the abuse. Looking for causes is also misleading because things that may look like causes — the parent's inability to control the teen — are often symptoms rather than causes.

## Today's World

Years ago, before home computers, television and movies, the world was very different. Teens spent most of their time with their families and their immediate neighbours and didn't travel far. Today, Canadian teenagers live in an exciting global village. From a young age, children go to daycare, watch television and movies and have home computers. As they grow older, at the touch of a few keys, they can access information from and about almost anywhere. From the world around them children learn about lifestyles and values. They learn how others live in this world and how they behave towards their parents. Although the dynamics in the home still play a major role, it is not helpful to target parents or focus on individuals without taking into consideration the broader social context. As a columnist wrote in a British social work magazine:

> our children across the classes and races are today beyond our control in the most profound sense. I do believe that the balance of forces has shifted dangerously as a result of this rampantly free market society so that the best parenting and the most appropriate schooling is still not enough to combat media images and expectations, peer group pressures, and the most destructive aspects of popular culture. Some children are driven, perhaps in spite of themselves, to antisocial and violent behaviour as a result of this environment, the long-term effects of which we will not know until it is too late. (Alibhai-Brown 2003: 22)

Mark Totten agrees. In his book, *Guys, Gangs and Girlfriend Abuse* (2000), he says that the sheer numbers of children who are violent and abusive means that the problem must be looked at from a sociological rather than an individual perspective. When we look more realistically at who should take responsibility for how children grow up, we see that it is a complex web. As social worker Jackie Barkley put it, "All adults are parenting the next generation, and community members of all kinds … share responsibility for what happens to our children" (personal communication).

Embedded in a child's development are the values of the culture in which they live, and while some are laudable, others are damaging. Both negative and positive values are expressed to our children by parents, extended families, social workers, teachers, police, store clerks, bus drivers, neighbours, adult friends, coaches, ministers — everyone with whom the teens come into contact. All these people parent our children and participate in giving them messages about how they should grow up in this world. Advertisers who bombard teens with advertising in a society that denies teens the economic opportunity to access material goods for themselves contribute to a frustrating and alienating culture for youth; the sales clerk who sides with teens in their struggle to have brand name sneakers is undermining the parent's authority; police who do not offer help when parents call undermine the parents' power. Canadian culture tends to value economic status more than it values caring for families. Women's work, especially their work as mothers, is disrespected instead of valued. When my daughter, for instance, told her boss that her child had caught head lice at daycare and she had to take the day off to care for her child, the boss, far from applauding her as a good mother, told her she wasn't valuing her work. But it is rare for anyone to pinpoint society's values and the way they are communicated to teens as a "cause" of teens' behaviour. Rather, individual, psychological explanations are given.

Although I do not advocate an approach that starts by looking for causes, I recognize and appreciate that parents sometimes find it helpful to identify anything that may be contributing to their teen's violence, as this helps them to move away from the guilt and despair they are feeling and to find a way to stop the abuse. At workshops I conduct, parents name what they think contributing factors may be. Because parents too focus on the psychological, individual contributors, their list usually includes:

- Family stress and parenting
- School problems
- Mental illness
- Learned behaviour
- Lack of information and community supports

It is important, as these are the contributors that parents name, that we discuss them. Previous chapters touched on most of these, and this chapter expands on the topics of family stress, school problems and mental illness. The next chapter is devoted to the issue of learned behaviour and lack of information and community supports.

## Family Stress

Family stress is first on the parents' list of causes, understandably so, because parenting teens in North America today can be extremely stressful. The way our society has evolved has made parenting more difficult. In today's market-driven world, parents are doing the vital and important work of raising the next generation, but they are given neither the recognition nor support they deserve. "[T]he whole world is pitted against [parents]," state Hewlett and West, whose book about the United States is also applicable to Canada. The authors name the "everyone" that is part of the conspiracy as "big business, government, and the wider culture," who, they believe, have secretly "waged a silent war against parents, undermining the work that they do" by "maximizing the economic and time pressures on parents, while the media do their level best to denigrate and displace moms and dads" (Hewlett 1998: 25). The result is that parents have been charged with an impossible mission, and, in Hewlett and West's words, even "adequate resources and a desperate desire to do a good job by our kids are no guarantee of success in this parent-hurting society" (Hewlett 1998: xiii-xv, 3).

In the past, community leaders, such as church elders, school teachers and police officers, had authority over us, and most of us believed that they were beyond reproach. Children were taught not to question or contradict them. Sadly, many secrets lay behind this façade and blind acceptance of community leaders led to many abuses. We have given teens good reason to doubt the wisdom of the older generation and we encourage them to question authority figures, including their parents. This is not necessarily a bad thing, but unfortunately many of their role models are disrespectful. Hollywood, for example, elevates teens at the expense of the adults they undermine, sending the clear message that children can control adults, and those who do are heroes. Insults and put-downs, lying and deceit are portrayed on sit-coms as normal and amusing family behaviour. A decade ago, Will Smith, who played an intelligent, charming young man in the *Fresh Prince of Bel Aire,* was made to look that way at the expense of his guardian, a wealthy, successful lawyer who was frequently outwitted by a teen. The *Home Alone* movies would have us believe that parents can be stupid enough to forget their children at home when they go on vacation and the children so clever they can outwit any adult. And so it goes on. In our attempt to take off the muzzle and expose the corruption of leaders, to give free speech and equal opportunity the rein they deserve, we have created a confusing world for teens. As a result, many teens are rootless and alienated, and teenage depression is becoming one of society's major concerns.

In his bold and compelling book, *Race Matters,* Cornel West writes about black teens growing up in the United States. Much of what he says about that society is relevant to all of us. West believes that society has lost its moral core and that teens have lost their hope. He places much of the blame on corporate market institutions, which have undermined traditional morality "in order to stay in business and make a profit" (1993: 26). Television and videos have reduced individuals to objects of pleasure. The images we are bombarded with are of "comfort, convenience, machismo, femininity, violence and sexual stimulation" (26). West has it right when he says, "These seductive images contribute to the predominance of the market-inspired way of life over all others and thereby edge out non-market values — love, care, service to others — handed down by preceding generations" (27). Our values are questionable. As Andy, one of the main characters in the Canadian novel, *Generation X,* says, we "spend our youth attaining wealth, and our wealth attaining youth" (Coupland 1991: 68). He questions these values and wonders why "we even bother to get up in the morning. I mean, really: why work? Simply to buy more stuff?" Later he says, "Our parents' generation seems neither able nor interested in understanding how marketers exploit them. They take shopping at face value," and he echoes many teens in his belief that history "has been turned into a press release, a marketing strategy, and a cynical campaign tool." It may be the breakdown in traditional values that, as West says, has created:

> the collapse of meaning in life — the eclipse of hope and absence of love of self and others, the breakdown of family and neighborhood bonds.... We have created rootless, dangling people with little link to the supportive networks — family, friends, school — that sustain some sense of purpose in life. (West 1993: 9)

Violence invades most corners of this uncertain life, and frequently it is presented not only as acceptable but to be applauded. In films and video games, on television and in everyday life, teenagers see that violence is commonly used to achieve goals and maintain control. Children bully each other, the police handle protesters roughly, Hollywood's good guys shoot and kill to save the world, politicians wage war to solve world problems. The list goes on. As one teen put it:

*Society is violent. Every day we hear about bomb threats and violent robberies and we see violence on television. Video games and comic books are full of violence. Violence is everywhere. Everyone's always fighting at school.*

Popular social and media messages include themes of violence against women, and teens learn through these social messages that it is acceptable for men and boys to control and dominate women and girls. The predominant message is that men are tough and rule the world; women are weak and powerless and do work that is less valuable than men's work. They only get respect when they act like men, so when women are portrayed as strong, they usually embody masculine images of power and are themselves violent. A great deal of debate concerns whether violence on television and in computer games causes children to be abusive. A recent publication which reviews some of the literature concludes, "Numerous studies have shown that watching violent television programs and films increases children's and adults' aggression and hostility; thus, it is plausible that playing violent computer games would have similar effects" (Subrahmanyam 2000: 133). It is difficult to believe that children are not affected in some way by the violence to which they are exposed. On the other hand, we should keep in mind that most children see television and computer game violence, but the majority are not abusive toward their parents. Although parents are given the burden of responsibility for the ways that society affects their teens, how can they counter this culture of violence?

## The Stress of Poverty

Most parents are struggling to raise their families alone. It is a dwindling minority of parents that have access to a supportive extended family and a tight-knit community. Money pressures leave parents with less and less time to spend with their children as they try to cope with modern day pressures of work without community support. Working long hours, travelling longer distances to work and worrying about money sucks everyone's energy and leaves parents too worn out and with too little time to devote to their teens. Parents suffer from what Sylvia Hewlett and Cornel West call "intense economic pressure" and "time famine" (1998: xv). This is especially so for the "working poor," who, in spite of all their efforts, do not have the financial resources they need to provide adequately for their families. To our shame, in a rich country like Canada, this is a huge number of families. In 1999, Statistics Canada revealed that 20 percent of the population owned 70 percent of the wealth, and 80 percent share the remaining. And these figures did not count in people living on reserves or in institutions or seniors' residences (Lee 2001: 2). Between 1984 and 1999, the poorest 40 percent of families saw little or no increase in their wealth, "while the richest of family units enjoyed increases in the order of 39 percent" (Kerstetter 2001: 1). What this means is that many of our families live in poverty. As Hewlett and West point out, at the time executives are being given bonuses in the millions of dollars, companies are laying off workers in the name of "efficiency" (1998: 32). And the gap between the rich and the poor continues to widen in both Canada and the U.S.

Poverty affects children from the time they are conceived. After separation or divorce, most women experience a drop in income, and as children usually live with their mothers, it may be that family poverty increases the potential for parent abuse to occur (Dornbusch 1985). Many pregnant women and mothers cannot afford to feed themselves and their children with healthy fruits and vegetables, and foods high in fat, salt and sugar, such as bologna and Kool-Aid, often comprise the diet of poor women and their children. An inadequate diet may not be a direct cause of parent abuse, but it is a cause of much ill health and, apart from anything else, it doesn't give people the vitality they need to cope with raising a family. Abusive children consume a great deal of time, which puts mothers who are scrambling to put food in the children's bellies in a quandary. The demands of low-wage jobs often mean that they, especially those who are parenting alone, work at the expense of their children.

It's a vicious cycle. The stress of dealing with limited resources often leads to increased tension and conflict in the family and depletes the parents so they have less energy to respond effectively in situations of conflict. Poverty breeds insecurity. It makes people fearful that they won't be able to cope, to pay the bills, to get by. It's difficult enough parenting teens anywhere, but poorer families may have no option but to live in dangerous neighbourhoods. These parents know their children are exposed to drugs and crime at a level they would not be exposed to in other areas of town and putting their children at risk adds to their sense of despair. The children feel this insecurity and despair and it robs them of a sense of safety. This in turn adds to the parents' depression and general sense of not being robust and healthy. Teenagers who grow up in families with very little money often have parents who don't spend much time with them, and the family doesn't have the resources for teens to take part in activities that interest them. This leads to the teens feeling alienated and resentful, and they take out their frustration and anger on their parents.

Lack of employment opportunities and the rising cost and standard of living has resulted in more teens living at home longer, or returning home after a short period of independence, than at any time in history. So, while they are working longer hours for less money at "McJobs" (Coupland 1991: 5) with little prestige, few benefits and no future, adults — more often women — are living with the stress of caring for and supporting their aging parents and their older children. Researchers tell us that this is a recipe for disaster. They have documented that in the animal kingdom, there is always more tension and fighting when young adults don't move out of the pack (Côté and Allahar 1994). Older teens, especially those who have left the home and returned, don't want to be treated like children. Although they are often not financially able to contribute to the household as adults, they feel they should have their independence, but no matter how hard everyone tries, "You can never be more than twelve years old with your parents," as *Generation X* Andy puts it (Coupland 1991: 137).

## Parenting in Today's World

To add to the stress, in today's world we all suffer from information overload. It is hard to watch television or read the newspapers without feeling inadequate in the face of world wars, starvation and the sadness of people's lives. Coupland's novel, *Generation X,* is about the alienation young people experience in a world that has, as Andy, says, "gotten too big." Youth can get overwhelmed by the violence and inequities in the world, and this adds to their struggles. At the same time, they learn about their rights as children. They are not always mature enough to understand that these laws are to protect them, not to use as weapons to threaten and intimidate their parents.

This leads us to questions about how parents can play a role in their teens' lives. It is clear that how we parent is not solely individual choice but is also influenced by the society we live in. Years ago children were considered the property of adults. They were expected to "be seen and not heard" and were often treated disrespectfully, or even cruelly, by adults both at home and in school. They had few rights, and parents were seldom held responsible for harming their children.

The permissive 1960s and the work to end child abuse changed much of that (Charles 1986). In *Power and Compassion,* Price (1996) outlines the impact of this on families. He explains that, although few people would dispute that children's rights must be recognized, attempts to protect these rights and to develop less authoritarian relationships have resulted in a parent-child power reversal that has led to a severe crisis in leadership within families. In an attempt to recognize children's basic need to have their feelings and opinions valued, this new way of child rearing shifted the focus away from the need for structure and leadership within the family. Kindness and an emphasis on the importance of a child's free expression of feelings became the central themes of positive parenting. Overall, the new child-centred approach resulted in significant benefits with respect to family functioning and children's emotional health, but in the extreme it also led to problems. Many parents came to believe that being loving, good parents meant being lenient. Coupled with this was the prevalent notion that all people's problems stem from growing up in "dysfunctional families." This may be part of the picture, but it begs the question of what is meant by "functional" and what kinds of supports are required for families to function well. Instead of being taken as a piece of the puzzle, it became society's mantra. Overwhelmed with this "knowledge" and not wanting to irreparably damage their children, parents stepped back from their leadership role. Most people will recognize these catch phrases that Price lists in his book:

> Children must make their own mistakes.
> If parents take charge, young people will never learn responsibility themselves.
> It's their life.
> Children must be trusted (whether they've earned that trust or not). Otherwise, the growth of the inner self will be stunted and creativity and self-expression thwarted.
> Young people have to make their own decisions (therefore, parents shouldn't force their judgment on young people.)
> A child's ego will be harmed if his or her right to total privacy is violated.
> It's intrusive to punish without giving advance warning as to the consequences. (1996: 18)

The notions above, and we have all tried to follow at least some of them, in fact discourage parents from exercising authority over their children. We have become a generation who put our energy into making teens comfortable instead of responsible. Many of us have succumbed to the changed role of the parent from authoritative disciplinarian to the other extreme of partners in an equal relationship, one in which parents are "friends" with their children. This can result in inappropriate and unhealthy parent/child relationships. One parent told me that it took time for her and her husband to realize that they couldn't be both friends and parents to their children. She wisely added that her children need parents to be parents, not their friends: "they have lots of friends out there." Parents need to exercise loving, compassionate leadership; they need to be neither overly harsh nor overly permissive.

This "equal" relationship places a burden on the teen as well. Children need to know their parents are in control and are the leaders in the family. They need what Haim Omer calls "a proper blend of firmness and love" (Omer 2000: xii). And they need to have clear boundaries and know the consequences of behaviour that steps over the line. A mother who tried to encourage the positive aspects of her son's personality, but without guidance, said it was disastrous: "My own lack of parenting him combined with Steve's temperament enabled him to be rebellious. I should've taken a much harder line with him but I encouraged his free spirit." It is normal for adolescents to go through a period of rebelling against parents' rules. But the parents' job is to enforce the rules. It's so much easier to give in, to offer friendship, but when parents are friends with their children, they often give the children too much leeway. The result is that children come to see parents as the people whose job it is to make them happy.

Having confidence in one's parenting style is not always easy. Parents are not encouraged to have faith in their common-sense instincts because parenting has become professionalized. Writers, psychologists, social workers and consultants set themselves up as "experts" on child rearing, and parents are pressured to consult these experts for advice and direction. Freud and Spock are two of the first and many "experts" who became famous for telling parents what they should and should not do. A huge and profitable publishing industry flourishes as books and magazines describe the terrible, lifelong impact of poor parenting on our children. Advertisers find it easy to convince parents that they should buy these books and, out of a fear of damaging their children forever, parents who have the resources do just that. The result of all the hype is that many parents, especially those who are having difficulties with their children, have lost faith in their ability to parent; they lack the confidence necessary to exert reasonable parental authority and take the leadership role in their families. Consequently, they don't give their children the guidance needed to grow up as responsible, moral teens and adults.

## The School's Response

These stresses are exacerbated when there are also problems with school. While schools are not a direct cause of parent abuse, they are rarely part of the solution either. Irene, for example, found the principal supportive, but felt the school was not equipped to handle her son's problems. In school, children quite appropriately are taught their rights, but parents feel that they are rarely taught their responsibilities and that children "got away with stuff" at school, like cursing and talking back to the teachers, being, as one mother said, "verbally abusive to the teachers." Irene said the school could do nothing when Colin refused to accept discipline at school or do his homework. Parents also felt that the children were not taught that their parents have the right to set limits on what they can and cannot do. Parents told us their interactions with school were often negative and they dreaded having contact with the school, partly because it was unpleasant to hear negative things about their children. Theresa echoed many parents when she said, "Parent teacher days were always hard. I remember that sinking feeling, sitting in front of each teacher not knowing what to expect." Parents also feel that schools erode their self-confidence and intensify the problems. While schools are quick to recognize how parents affect their children, they generally ignore the ways in which the schools affect parents and parent-child interactions. The message is usually that parents should take responsibility for their children's behaviour at school. This is easier said than done. I remember one teacher asking me what I was going to do about the fact that my daughter wouldn't speak up in French class. I was tempted to say, "Nothing. I'm not there. You are." Instead, I asked what she would suggest. She thought I should talk to my daughter about it. It seemed odd to me that this was considered the parent's task and not the teacher's. Parents dread talking to teachers and principals, because teachers often act as though they alone know what is best. They scapegoat the parent by blaming them for the child's misbehaviour. One abused mother said that she had "the principal coming down on me saying it was my responsibility to get my kid to school." Teachers blamed Theresa's son's behaviour on her divorce. What became clear in my research is that schools also tend to hold the parents responsible for finding a solution. Catherine summed it up in a letter to me: "School officials just wanted the problem to go away and falsely believed I had some power in that regard."

## Mental Illness

The last of the "causes" we examine in this chapter is mental illness. Studies on parent abuse state that the majority of teens who abuse their parents are not emotionally ill. However, some abusive teens are, and of those, the majority are clinically diagnosed with ADHD and behaviour disorders, but some are ill with schizophrenia or bipolar disorder. Unfortunately, these latter illnesses are difficult to diagnose, and appropriate professional intervention often doesn't occur until after a lengthy period of behaviour problems. The mother of a schizophrenic teen said she dragged her son to every specialist and expert she could find, but they all thought her parenting was to blame for his behaviour, and only after "years of hell" was his illness diagnosed. Having the teen's condition labelled by a psychiatrist helps some parents understand their child's behaviour. One mother said she thought her son was being manipulative and was angry with him, until he became extremely ill and was diagnosed as schizophrenic. It helped her to have the psychiatrist explain that teens with schizophrenia are very difficult people to deal with, and that, "These young men are not stupid or evil. They are isolated and withdrawn and suffer from terrible loneliness."

Having a psychiatrist confirm that the teen is seriously mentally ill can be a relief, because finally parents can explain their teens' behaviour and they can let go of the crushing guilt and blame they have been living with. However, the relief is short-lived because it soon becomes apparent to the parents that there is little hope and they are going to be dealing with a very difficult issue for a long time.

Getting a diagnosis for less serious mental illnesses — these are listed in Chapter Six — is seldom difficult and can be helpful because it qualifies the teens and their parents for free counselling at mental health clinics. In these days of cutbacks to social services and a chronic lack of community mental health services, parents are eager to access counselling wherever they can get it. Without the diagnosis, mental health professionals consider parent abuse a safety issue, not a mental illness; they refuse to accept the families and refer them to the justice system. It is unfortunate that in order to access counselling services, teens have to be labelled mentally ill, rather than simply having their behaviour labelled. It's what Price calls the "mad/bad dichotomy." Pathologizing parent abuse, that is, giving it a name as a mental illness or disorder, can be destructive. For one thing, it can reduce any hope for change. "I have ADHD or a conduct disorder" essentializes the teen. For another, while these diagnoses identify a problem, without attention to the teen's behaviour, they are merely labels of the symptoms and, therefore, not very helpful. For example, abusive teens are frequently diagnosed as having a conduct disorder. But precisely what does that mean? When a child is out of a parent's control and is behaving abusively, it doesn't take an expert to see that the child's behaviour, or "conduct," is not in order, or to put it in psychiatry-speak, is "disordered." There is also the danger that these labels may eventually become self-fulfilling. As Price says,

> When adults overreact to children's symptoms with diagnoses and hospitalizations, children learn from their reflection in the eyes of parents and therapists, who they are now and what they're going to become. Children either identify themselves as sick or believe themselves to be normal people with problems that can be solved. If their reflection is of a disordered person, they are less likely to get better and exhibit more normal behaviour. (Price 1996: 43)

Labelling can result in the teens being stigmatized at school and by their peers, and it can also be used to excuse certain behaviours and create further problems. Price cautions parents not to let labels or diagnoses frighten them into believing they cannot expect to be treated respectfully by their children. They have a right to expect decent behaviour, however ill their children are. Children must be expected to treat people properly if they're ever to improve.

Psychiatrists prescribe medication where they deem it appropriate. There are pros and cons to this. The drugs can help control aggressive behaviours, as this mother confirms: "Once he was diagnosed and put on the medication it was like he stopped. He didn't hit anymore, he didn't throw the fits anymore, he started to identify with himself, so the medication stabilizes his aggression." Another mother said that after her son started taking medication, he realized that he had been physically abusive towards her and was upset and angry with himself for it. But for many parents prescription drug use among teens is a concern because it can lead to another serious problem: drug abuse. Mothers told us they have to be vigilant about the drugs their children are taking. One mother explained: "They're on Dexedrine for ADHD and I give it to them every day, because I know what can happen if they get hold of it." More than one mother of an abusive child reported that their teens sold the Ritalin. Theresa says Ritalin left her son in a fog, and Irene said she had to struggle with her son to get him to take it. Price is also concerned about drug use, especially for children with schizophrenia, and cautions parents:

> The greatest danger of a diagnosis of schizophrenia in a child is the use of psychotropic medications and the accompanying risk of neurological damage from them. Any professional applying such a diagnosis to a child should be viewed with a great deal of suspicion, and a second opinion should be sought. (Price 1996: 51)

## Conclusion

Parenting in today's world of globalization and rapid social change can be extremely stressful because, although teens are influenced by social dynamics that are out of their parents' control, parents are held responsible for their teens' behaviour. As well as family dynamics and individual characteristics, gender, race, class, ability, religion and societal and cultural values all come into play. In this morass of influences, it is impossible to find isolated "causes" of parent abuse, and, at best, we can say that we can identify dynamics that contribute to abuse. To suggest that the victims are solely to blame for the abuse they suffer is a gross over-simplification. This fact should stop us from holding parents totally to blame for their teens' behaviour and for stopping the abuse. They already feel stressed, unsupported and struggling and do not need this extra burden. Instead of jumping to conclusions and blaming parents, instead of driving them crazy questioning where they went wrong, there are more healthy ways we can use to stop parent abuse.

We can start by having more understanding of their struggles. Parents need to be respected for doing their compassionate best. They need to be supported in having confidence that it is they, not the "experts" or the writers of magazine articles, who know what their families need. Whether we are parents or not, we need to stop focusing on who did what wrong and start working together to support each other and help raise the next generation.

Whatever the dynamics, there is no excuse for the violence. It is every parent's right to live in safety, to exercise loving authority over their children and to encourage their children to be as responsible as they are happy. In order for them to feel secure, teens need this as much as their parents. And ultimately, it is the teens who must make changes, learn to accept responsibility for their behaviour and exercise self-control. The next chapter looks at the supports available to parents who are attempting to work with their teens to end the abuse.

# 9. Information and Supports

*We tried everywhere and no one could help us. Unless they have been there too, friends and family and even the professionals can't understand the pain you feel.*

When abuse first begins, many parents can't accept that their children *could* be abusive toward them. They refuse to admit it to themselves. Eventually, though, it becomes such a problem that they do begin to suspect that they are being victimized. At that point they begin to doubt themselves and question their ability to parent. Sometimes this introspection helps them to understand the family dynamic and develop strategies to control the child's behaviour, but usually it immobilizes them. Caught up in a guilty search for what they've done wrong, they can't act. Admitting to the abuse makes them feel like failures, and often, when they share their awful secret with others, this feeling is confirmed.

Parents play a major role in their children's development, but, as we discussed earlier, society plays a pivotal role in creating and perpetuating abusive behaviour. Instead of acknowledging this and taking collective responsibility for our teens, it is the parents we blame when things go wrong. The belief that parents are the sole influence on their children places an impossible load of responsibility on parents' shoulders. Parents, along with everyone else, buy into this belief and often take full responsibility for their teen's actions. They avoid talking to family and friends or to professional service providers because they know they will receive blaming messages. They are told that their teens are abusing them because they are over-controlling or under-controlling and that they need to put boundaries in place — even though the abuse typically occurs precisely when they do just that. Feeling blamed and solely responsible makes it difficult for parents to get past their feelings of failure and shame so they can hear positive and useful suggestions to change their behaviour.

## Breaking the Silence

Challenging the belief that parents are the sole influence on their children can be refreshing for parents. In order to do this, parents have to break their silence. Finding listeners who do not judge them can be a huge relief and often the beginning of the end of the abuse. A few months after she had been interviewed for the 1995 study, a woman told me that, while talking about her relationship with her daughter, she realized she was responding to her daughter's abusive behaviour with feelings of mother-shame: guilt and responsibility for being a "bad mother." While telling her story she began to see it wasn't all her fault, and from that moment she was able to begin to handle her daughter with more distance and authority. She felt stronger because she was finding her own way, her own solutions; she just needed the little support she received from the interview. A number of other women we interviewed were relieved to have the opportunity to talk about their experiences with their abusive teens in a non-judgmental, supportive environment. By taking part in the research, these women realized they weren't alone in parenting an out-of-control teenager. That made it easier for them to name the abuse and begin to understand the dynamics at play, and then to take the steps necessary for change so they could regain control. One mother told me that the interview helped her recognize that she had thought she was feeling shame but in fact she was deeply sad, and there is a big difference between the two. Another said that once she recognized she was being abused and did not have to "put up with it," she could get "unhooked" and emotionally separate from her child.

When they begin to shift the focus to their own needs, parents sometimes recognize that their response to their teen's abuse is abusive or needy. They are then able to end the abusive cycle by using more positive communication strategies and by not letting their own need for harmony and love, or their anger, interfere. These parents need a great deal of support and understanding. They know that keeping the abuse secret from others, especially other family members, teaches teens that their actions will remain secret and entrenches the abusive behavior. They need support to address their feelings of failure and helplessness and to unpack the influences of guilt and blame, so that they can move forward. But disclosing their situation to others is risky, because not only are they vulnerable to judgment, they are often afraid that their teen will hear about it, and this will incite further incidents of abuse against them.

Even when they have overcome their fear, admitted the abuse to themselves and decided to talk about it, it is not easy for parents to find help. Lori described her experience:

> *I work in the community and I've lived here for fifteen years and know*
> *many people, but I feel the community has turned on me. Christopher has*
> *done a lot of damage and said a lot of horrible things about people. It's really*
> *hard. People who always talked to me, or our kids went to school since they*
> *were little and have gone to class trips together, they actually avoid me and*
> *don't even speak to me. They just walk by. It's a huge emotional strain.*

There are few places where parents feel safe enough to talk about what is happening and few options and ideas for what they can do. They are caught in a spiral of deepening shame and despair at the very time they need to be strong enough to deal with the abusive teen. As Linda said, "Here I was, a person that my clients looked to for advice, and I didn't know which way to turn." This futile search for support leaves parents with diminished hope and an increased sense of failure. The result is they become even less able to cope. Although sometimes they do find friends, family or a service agency willing to help, parents often feel worse than they did before they shared their stories. Potentially supportive people fail because they are not informed about the issue. They think the abuse is the parents' fault and are quick to judge when parents speak about their pain.

Parents often end up feeling more blamed than helped and wish they had remained silent. Lori says that people are often critical of her husband and ask why he doesn't "do something,'" but, she asks, "What do they want him to do?" Supportive people tire of hearing about the topic and "burn out" as listeners, or they offer advice and refuse to listen any longer when they see that their advice is not taken. Unless one has lived it, this problem can be very difficult to understand. Lori says that a common response is, "If that was my kid, I'd kill him" or they say they'd throw him out. She asks, "Throw him out where? Child welfare have no place. When it's your child there are no limitations to love." Linda's colleagues knew about her son's behaviour, but she didn't want to ask them for help because she had often heard them explain children's bad behaviour as the result of poor parenting practices and lack of boundaries. Because she is a professional, well-educated woman, they thought she should be able to handle things better and couldn't understand how she could let this happen. She felt as if she had BAD PARENT stamped on her forehead.

Condemnation is the response when parents "allow the abuse" and also when they don't. Mary experienced this when, in a radio interview, she stated that, after years of suffering abuse at the hands of her teenage daughter, she sometimes found it difficult to love her daughter. Although she had used a false name to protect her daughter, her colleagues heard the broadcast and recognized her voice. Their response was to criticize her about speaking publicly and for being "so cold and uncaring." They did not understand how a mother could ever "give up" on her child and were shocked that Mary was so "hard." Their hurtful response was devastating and did not encourage Mary to talk about her struggles again. Her colleagues' reaction made Mary feel somehow she'd betrayed herself and her family. No one wants others thinking badly of them or their family, and feelings of love and family loyalty prevent many parents from looking for the support they need. Connie said she felt dreadful talking negatively about her own daughter when she had to tell her story to the police. These parents desperately need support. They continue to look for it, and continue to be disappointed.

## The Helping Professionals

The severe lack of appropriate resources to help parents is a constant frustration. This mother echoes many others:

> I called everyone in the phone book that I thought could have helped. I exhausted every avenue I could think of exhausting. There's a considerable lack of resources for parents of children this age. They are very, very under serviced.

When they reach out for help, parents are often desperate and in situations which require immediate attention. What they often find is overburdened resources with long waiting periods. The response time for assistance is far too long. In addition, agencies have specific requirements that exclude many families. Many mental health agencies refuse to handle these cases, and child protection agencies usually do not accept them either. Even where services are available, they are not always accessible. Sometimes lack of transportation is a barrier, and parents are not always able to leave the teen unsupervised.

Parents who manage to find professional service providers in the child welfare, justice and mental health systems who will talk to them are often disappointed with the response. This dissatisfaction is not unfounded. Healing "disordered" children is the task of professionals, but they tend to put full responsibility on the parents, not just for the abuse they experience, but also to find a cause and a cure. They imply that it is the parents who need to change their behaviours, attitudes and parenting practices, often in ways the parents can't relate to, and, ultimately, put the onus on the parents to stop the misbehaviour. This appears to parents as mother-blaming. Although many counsellors are dedicated professionals, there is a problem within the system. Omer summed it up this way:

> I believe that parents have often been treated unkindly by the helping professions. They have been made to take the blame for every problem posed or faced by their children. They have been accused of servicing their own egotistic ends rather than the needs of their children. They have been routinely described as lacking in empathy and sensitivity and as having only minimal understanding of their children. ( 2000: x)

## Mental Health Professionals

One of the reasons service providers blame the parents is that, more often than not, they believe that all psychological problems have their roots in childhood experiences. In part, this Freudian perspective is prevalent because most counsellors come out of a psychology or social work, background. Thus, they see the parent as responsible for causing the child's behaviour and feel it is only fitting that parents should bear the burden of repairing the damage. Therapists label parents who are reluctant to change as "unmotivated," "not up to the task" or "unfit for parenting," but Omer believes:

> these negative characterizations of parents are more reflective of our helplessness as therapists rather than the parents' true condition. In no small degree, we therapists are responsible for our own negative views. Correcting them and evolving an attitude of respect for parents may well be the first crucial step in the treatment. ( 2000: 34)

Parents have horror stories to tell about mental health professionals' unhelpful attitudes. Lori's sad words tell us a great deal:

*I feel so awful after I leave the counsellor's office. I cry all the way home. I am such a mess, I go to my family doctor on a regular basis and he usually makes me feel better. He says, "I've known you since you were sixteen and*

*I know you're a good person, and if somebody's making you feel you're not, don't listen to them. Just because they're in the profession it doesn't mean they know. They don't know you and they don't know everything."*

Theresa and her husband had more than one bad experience. Theresa says the words, "there is no such thing as a problem child, just problem parenting" still ring in her ears, and adds, "How awfully cruel some therapists can be." In one session they were asked to pick out their son's characteristics from a psychologist's list, and, based on that, David was diagnosed as a psychopath. They were, of course, in shock, but were given little advice on how to respond. Another therapist told Theresa her son was abusing her because he was bored and hyperactive and suggested David should have a diet free of preservatives and colourants. Good advice for anyone, but it is unlikely to stop parent abuse, and following it can consume a great deal of time most parents, especially abused parents, don't have. Some parents are frustrated by the advice and treatment they receive:

*When I moved here [he] was six weeks old and then I started seeing some weird stuff. And I was going to doctors here who said; "Oh no — it's just because he needs a dad." So I was really starting to think I was going crazy and stuff. And you'd think that if he has such a hard time if it's a dad situation or whatever, then how come my other two children weren't going the same way?*

Another parent was also disappointed with the psychiatrist's response to her son:

*I was seeing a psychiatrist out here [who] had asked me at some point how old I was. And then he told me I was still young enough to have more children. Basically, [my son] was a "write-off." And I thought; "I don't need this — for someone to be telling me to give up on my son."*

The attribution of blame takes many forms. My friend Catherine was told that her daughter was abusing her because she is lesbian.

Another problem is that not all mental health professionals address the child's abusive behaviour towards the parents. This is one mother's experience:

*We worked with one psychiatrist who did not in any way address the abuse issues.... We repeatedly brought up the issue of violence because it was escalating. As the violence continued to worsen, I was told to call the police and the situation was never looked at comprehensively and in depth. Not only do they not get it, but they make it worse.... We started working with another psychiatrist but she didn't address the abuse issues either. At that point my daughter was locking me in closets, putting her fists through walls and raging on a daily basis. And that went on for a year and a half.*

Counselling sessions with their teens, when they can get them to attend them — and that can be a major struggle — can be extremely uncomfortable for parents. Zelda's teens resented her sharing her story with others. Teens who are abusive know they have power over their parents and will try to manipulate the counsellor into siding with them and blaming the parent for the abuse. Linda's son, Robert, presented himself and the situation in such a way that it looked as though everything was Linda's fault, leaving Linda feeling even worse than she did already. "Worse" is how many parents feel after counselling. This is extremely unhelpful and can be damaging.

Because parents are expecting to be blamed for their teens' abusive behaviour, they may see blame where none was intended. Psychologist Eddie Gallagher points out:

> We need to be aware that what some see as simply gathering information, may be taken by many parents as implying guilt. Parents may see questions such as: "was he a planned child?"; "did you work when he was a baby?" as implying that he was unloved or neglected. Since the answers to such questions seldom have any useful effect on what we actually do with a family, such detailed history taking can be a dangerous habit. (Gallagher 2004)

## Criminal Justice Professionals

The judicial system is not structured to deal effectively with parent abuse cases. It is adversarial and does not function well in dealing with these types of abusive relationships, so parents are often reluctant to take the huge step of getting involved in it. They are torn because they know they have to stop the abuse, but they don't want their child to go through the system and have a criminal record. In my own research, the police are named most often as the "most helpful" service providers that parents consulted. Unfortunately, they are also named most often as the least helpful. When Lori called the police for help they suggested she get her son to sign a contract. They said that if he violated the contract, she should call them and they would return. Christopher didn't keep to the rules, but when Lori called the police, they refused to come:

> *So what they did was threaten him but not follow through. That's the worst thing you can do with a child with a conduct disorder.... What they did was show him that it doesn't matter anyway. I haven't called them again because I'm so tired of calling people and talking to them and nothing ever comes out of it. It's just a waste of time.*

Police response tends to be inconsistent because few police forces have protocols for dealing with parent abuse. Whether they are helpful or not often depends on the personal styles of the individual officers and how aware they are of the complexity of the situation. One parent said, "Each time was different. It depended on which cop showed up." But there are few alternatives when parents are seriously afraid for their safety. Connie was lucky. A passerby called the police when she saw Connie being kicked by her daughter, and the officer who came was sympathetic and kind. He acknowledged the seriousness of the assault, reassured her she was not alone, that others, including the officer himself, experienced such things. He gave Connie the option of having the teen charged and left his card urging her to call if she ever needed help again.

Police involvement can help teens understand the seriousness of their behaviour, and just knowing their parents will call the police can be enough to motivate them to curb the abuse and avoid the consequences. Connie's husband wanted assault charges laid against their daughter, but Connie wanted to give her another chance because she knew that having a criminal record could affect the teen's whole life. Facing the decision was extremely difficult because they knew "it could be worse the next time if we don't do it this time. She could end up being very violent and something really bad could happen."

Another mother said that she called the police on a number of occasions when she felt she was in danger. The responding officer talked to her daughter and struck a perfect balance between being strict and compassionate. He confronted the teen in front of her mother, laid out the consequences if the abuse didn't stop and told her she was violating her mother's essential rights as a human being. With the threat hanging over her of being charged with assault and disturbing the peace, or with being placed in a group home, the abuse diminished. From that time, when she was beginning to be abused, the mother would move to the phone. That gesture kept the teen from actually hitting her on a number of occasions.

Parents are often afraid that the situation will get worse if they call the police. This is not an unrealistic fear. Sometimes the police minimize the teen's behaviour and refer to it as a "family fight." One couple called the police when the teen stole their car, and the officer said, "I'm sure he just borrowed it." Another mother said:

> My daughter hit me twice while she was on probation for assault. Both times I called the police and they wouldn't come. When they do come they don't do anything for parents. They laugh, they think it's a joke. They have no idea how to work with abused parents.

One mother called the police when her daughter assaulted her, and the officer asked, "Don't you have a husband there that can take care of this?" These experiences contribute to a sense of hopelessness and discourage parents from seeking assistance in the future. An ineffective response from the criminal justice system can reinforce youth violence against parents. In these cases, the teen recognized that there were minimal consequences and in some cases felt that this condoned the violence:

> The court, it all depends on what judge you get. Some judges think; "Let's just let the kid go home and he'll be okay." Other judges look at it and; "You've done all this in this period of time. No — we've had enough."

> They picked her up and she spent the night in jail and ... she was put on probation. Unfortunately, things with kids are so easy that they also quickly learn that they can do it hundreds of times and nothing much happens.

Many assault charges carry with them the mandate that perpetrators must not go near the victim, but in parent abuse cases this is clearly problematic because the victim is responsible for the perpetrator. Some parents regret involving the criminal justice system because they find it even more difficult to live with the teen after assault charges are laid.

The system is often slow: cases can take more than a year to come to court, and the victim usually has to live with the teen in a tense state of limbo not knowing what the outcome will be. The justice system's failure to enforce quick and meaningful consequences further entrenches the abuse. When the courts do eventually respond, the teens' punishment can be as hard on the mother as the teen. Jordan was put under house arrest. The untenable consequence was that mother and son, the victim and the perpetrator, were confined together in their small apartment, day in, day out. It does appear, however, that it taught him a lesson. He doesn't like the way he is having to live, hates being under house arrest and says he will stay out of trouble in future. Two teens told Peter Monk, a social worker in British Columbia, that the threat of further jail time or probation also makes them want to change. One said:

> *And now I am on probation for a very, very long time — which I just found out. And having to learn the hard way, and being tied down.... But I don't ever want to go back to [youth custody] again so I have been trying to be good. (Monk 1997: 12)*

The general lack of information about parent abuse results in many parents having unrealistic expectations of the justice system. There are limits to what the police can do. The justice system functions with clear parameters and is mandated to respond to criminal behaviour, such as physical abuse, threats, theft and damage to property. While some forms of parent abuse are difficult for parents to live with, they do not necessarily constitute an offence under the *Criminal Code*. The job of the police is to deal with immediate situations, and they can rarely be involved in helping parents find long-term solutions.

According to a number of parents, court orders to attend school or stay at home and follow the rules are seldom supervised or enforced, and probation officers are overworked and cannot properly supervise the children under their care. Like this mother, few parents have much trust in the criminal justice system:

> *I had her charged. She got eight months probation and community service, and she had certain restrictions and conditions like she had to go to school and she wasn't to hit me. She violated every condition of her probation and they did nothing. I told the probation officer she hit me. I only got involved with the justice system because I wanted her forced to go into therapy. I didn't want her charged. I wanted her in therapy. The police and the prosecutor said, "Charge her, it's the best way to get her into therapy." Here we are, six months later, and still no therapy. They lied to me.*

Victims are eligible for criminal injuries counselling, but their applications for help take months to process, and the service is strictly for victims. Parents need help more immediately, and most want to include the perpetrator, their child, in the counselling.

Parents can also feel less in control and more vulnerable when the police and the court system are involved. African Canadian, immigrant or gay parents — in fact any parents who are not white, middle-class and heterosexual — may be afraid to seek help from agencies such as the police for fear the child will be subjected to racism, homophobia or other forms of discrimination.

## Child Welfare Workers

Parents fare no better when they contact child welfare agencies looking for help. Support is usually denied because child welfare agencies are not mandated to deal with cases of parent abuse. As it is the parent, not the child, who is the victim of abuse, the child is not in need of child welfare intervention. The agencies are obligated to investigate if there are other children in the home and assess if they are at risk from their sibling. Donna's least abusive daughter was put in a group home to protect her from her sister, and her more abusive sister was left at home for her parents to cope with. Another problem is that child welfare intervention is reactive. They focus on immediate risks and do not offer prevention services unless they believe there is a risk of harm to the teen. However, most abused parents argue that abusive teens, who do not control their anger, may indeed place themselves in situations where they are at risk and, therefore, are in need of protection.

Some parents are reluctant to contact child welfare services, because they are afraid that the teen will be removed from the home, and they fear the loss of emotional connection if this happens. These fears are even stronger in single-parent families where the teen is an only child or in cases where the teen is also a parent and there is the potential loss of contact with a grandchild. Others want the child removed from the home. As one child welfare supervisor put it, "Most parents cannot understand how their teen turned from a sweet little child into a "monster." They call child welfare to take the teen and teach them a lesson or fix them." One mother wanted her daughter taken into care because anxiety about the girl's safety was making her ill:

*I almost ended up in the psychiatric hospital. I wouldn't answer the door, the phone. I had someone escort the other children to school. I got sick if the police came by and I wouldn't open the door. I was an emotional wreck because of concern for her — afraid that the police were coming to tell me that my daughter was dead. I begged social services to put her somewhere in a confined area where she couldn't just get up and go where she wanted. I'm so scared to death for her life. I think the only thing that's going to help her is a secure environment where she can't just say "Screw you, I'm going."*

But there are not enough alternative homes available to make possible the removal of abusive children from their homes, and the few parents who do get their children into care often regret the decision as child welfare has no "cure" for these teens. Teens are rarely placed in foster care; they are placed in a group home. Group homes do not have "secure" rooms or any way to stop the teen from leaving, so teens quickly learn that they can come and go whenever they like. There are few treatment programs or controls to contain aggressive behaviour in a group home, other than contacting the police and having the teen charged, which are the very same controls the parents have. As well, teens get to know other teens with similar behaviours and may become even more defiant.

Having their teen in care can create additional problems for the family. Sometimes the government financial assistance teens receive while in care provides the teen with more freedom and financial support than their parent are willing or able to provide. This can result in the teen rebelling against the rules and limitations of the family home upon their return. One mother said she felt her daughter was laughing because she was getting what she wanted: "While she's in foster care they're taking her out shopping for clothes and to the eye doctor and dentist, all the stuff that I can't afford on family benefits. She gets to come and go more there too. I think that is sending a really bad message to her." This mother had a similar problem:

*Jenny ran away from home and went to a group home. A pattern started. They kept her for two weeks and gave her a steady allowance, $300 in clothing allowance. I blame a lot on [the child welfare] system because they bought her nice clothes, stuff that I couldn't afford. That's when a pattern developed. She'd come back home and things would be fine. She'd want something I couldn't afford, then she'd become defiant, not do her homework, fight with [the other] kids and with me. She would constantly fight or throw dishes at me or on floor.*

Another mother said:

> [The child welfare agency] made it hard for us to reunite because they gave him too much. They spoiled him. He lived in a fantasy land. You've got to teach him rules, regulations, that's how the world is. Now with me, I've got nothing, I can't give him everything he wants.

It also causes problems with the teen's siblings:

> It was also confusing for the other children. She would flaunt the new clothes she bought with her children's aid allowance in front of them. It really bothered me. She was getting all these things I couldn't afford for my other kids because she could play the system.

Mothers who finally succeeded in having their teens placed in foster care for a short period sometimes find they are less able to cope when the teen returns home:

> I had gotten used to the low stress life I had while he was out of the home, and when he returned his behavior was too much. We argued about everything. He made it seem like he was cooperating, but would at the same time try to get away with things. I gave a lot of privileges that I wouldn't have if he hadn't been in control, like he had developed a lot of adult habits. The going away and coming back made the problem worse.

Lack of follow-up from social workers when the teen returns home is a problem and, if the abuse begins again, parents feel unsupported. Follow-up is essential, especially when a number of agencies are involved. In this family, the parents were given contradictory messages:

> There was a no-contact order instituted by the judge, [so] legally he couldn't come home. We were sort of stuck in the middle. We were told by the probation officer and the social worker he had to come home — they refused to provide a home for him.

## The "Hot Potato" Routine

Service providers are often unable to help and instead add to the parents' distress by sending them off on a "wild goose chase" from one agency to another. The police refer the parents to child welfare agencies; child welfare workers think it is a criminal matter that should be dealt with by the justice system, and refer the parents back to the police. As one child welfare supervisor admitted, "Child welfare does not accept these families and we deflect them to some other agency if we can." If a child is using drugs, the family may be referred to a drug addiction agency. Parents refer to this as the "hot potato routine." One mother said for over five years she searched for help and kept "running into brick walls" as she tried vainly to get help with her daughter, who continued to steal from her, lie and assault her. Child welfare didn't know where to send her because she had already accessed every service available: social workers and counsellors, the family doctor, a pediatrician and a psychiatrist, student support workers and school psychologists. Theresa said that her child's teachers "passed the buck" and urged her to consult a therapist about her son. She took their advice because she felt guilty that her son had witnessed her "ugly divorce," but it only succeeded in increasing her self-doubt and causing her to spend yet more time and money without providing any solution to the problem.

Running from one service agency to another is tiring and time-consuming. There can be weeks when every day is taken up with appointments with lawyers, doctors and counsellors, as well as court appearances. One mother said she could not go out and look for work because she was so tied up with the aftermath of her attempts to stop the abuse. And not finding support leaves parents feeling helpless and hopeless. As Theresa put it:

> The real crux of the matter is: where do you go to for help? Real help. It's so hard. Being in the middle of a crisis in Nova Scotia is like being in the desert with no water; you just know you are dying and no one is going to come and help you. The police tell you to call your doctor; the doctors put you on Prozac; the agencies and the hospitals all have huge waiting lists.

Service providers agree that there is a failure in the system. A great deal of public money and time is spent providing services for families, particularly by the provincial departments of Community Services, Health and Justice, but parents experiencing parent abuse aren't finding the help they need. A mother who lives in an isolated rural community discovered how the system fails. For a long time, like most parents, she kept secret the abuse she was suffering at the hands of her teenage son, until one day, worn down and ashamed and in fear for her life, she dialled 911. There ensued months of intervention by justice, child welfare and mental health services. Finally the boy was sent to a juvenile facility where, presumably, he will harden, and the mother was left alone feeling a total failure. Parents' inability to access adequate support certainly contributes to the continuation and escalation of the abuse.

## Success!

In spite of this gloom, there are some success stories. The Mi'kmaq Family Healing Centre in Nova Scotia held a weekend retreat for mothers and their teenage daughters, where for two days, mothers and daughters talked, played, ate and enjoyed each other. Everyone felt a new intimacy, a new connection, and the evaluations were glowing. This short event went a long way to reducing abuse in these families. There are also some community healing programs in place. Roots of Empathy and Leave Out Violence Everywhere (LOVE) are two that attempt to build caring, peaceful and civil societies. Roots of Empathy began in two schools in Toronto in 1996 and is now in over 140 schools in seven provinces. It aims to reduce aggression and violence by helping children see another person's point of view, think about others' feelings and talk about caring relationships. The LOVE Program is another highly successful attempt to give teens an opportunity to learn self-worth and respect for others. Through photojournalism and video making, the teens are given the tools to turn ugly emotions into something beautiful. It is worth trying to find out if any programs like these are operating locally.

## Conclusion

On the whole, the situation for abused parents is bleak. Someone once said, "I'm not a pessimist, I'm a realist," and this chapter is realistically dismal with few hopeful moments. Parent abuse persists because of the secretiveness around it, the lack of understanding of the issue and the incessant blaming of the victim. As Lori said, "When people see a child out of control, they always look at the mother and say, 'Hmmm, I wonder what's going on in that home.'" She admits that she was one of those people who judged others, and only after experiencing abuse herself does she say, "I don't do that any more."

Parents are held solely responsible for the cause and the cure, and for caring for their teens while they are being abused. Most abused parents try "the whole gamut" of support services and devote years of their lives waiting for appointments and attending them. But, in the words of one parent, "nothing works," and not finding the help they need, they are left with an increased sense of isolation, shame and futility. There are, however, some things parents can do. These are discussed in the next chapter.

# 10. Supportive Listeners

We therapists had better learn how to help these families because the support systems are failing them. (Jerome Price)

Parents can make healthy decisions about their lives and act on those decisions to begin the long and difficult process of ending the abuse, but most have run out of ideas and solutions and energy, and they need encouragement and support. They need one supportive person in their lives with whom they feel safe and who will listen and not minimize the problem or make them feel worse than they already do. Sadly, understanding and support are, as we saw in Chapter Nine, in short supply. Parents have to know the ropes and actively search to find help. Support can come in the form of a non-professional, such as a friend or relative, a volunteer or even another parent, but parents should beware: without appropriate training, people may have difficulty listening to this topic, especially if they have had similar experiences. A volunteer lay-counsellor at a church told me she was shocked when she found herself responding with feelings of anger to a parishioner who talked about her abusive son, and it took some time for the lay-counsellor to realize that the situation mirrored her brother's abuse of her mother. She had never realized how angry she was with her mother for enduring the abuse and wisely withdrew from counselling until she had dealt with her own feelings. Although they do not always succeed, professional counsellors are trained to avoid identifying with others. It is worth stating again that non-professionals often feel they have to find a solution to the problem, and they get frustrated when parents don't take their advice. They can also be highly judgmental and tend to tire of hearing about the situation and have trouble hanging in for the long haul.

## Parent Support Groups

Parent groups can offer significant support by sharing stories, strategies and suggestions for where to get help. In a successful group, parents feel supported and not judged and gain strength from knowing they are not alone in their struggles. One parent said of her group: "They listen to me. They support me. They know I can only do what I can do." Support groups also offer the opportunity for parents to help others, which can challenge parents' feelings of helplessness about their own abusive situation. But to be worthwhile, the group has to feel right for the parents, and that often depends on how well the parent "fits" with the other members. In some groups, members may have to agree with only one philosophy and may not be "allowed" their own opinions. For example, the emphasis in some groups is for parents to support each other in, as one parent put it, "kicking the kids out of the home." But some parents may be uncomfortable with this, because finding a safe place for their teens to go is not easy and they are not always prepared to put their teens at risk. "Our home is the safest place for our abusive kids," one parent said. Another parent found support group meetings, "too tough, not spiritual enough." Groups are sometimes dominated by the parents with the most dramatic stories, and this can scare away those who need preventive help. There can also be a tendency for members to tell their stories over and over again without making any attempt to change the situation, and this can promote the attitude that the situation and the teens are hopeless. People attend support groups because they are under a lot of stress at home, and it is not surprising that this stress sometimes spills over into the group in destructive ways. It is often conflictual inter-personal dynamics that lead to the groups' demise. The best support groups are often facilitated by a professional who can help parents move beyond their anger and despair. Unfortunately, few support groups exist, and those that do receive little or no support, financial or otherwise, from governments or professionals. Parents get burned out just trying to keep the groups active and positive.

## Mediation, Restorative Justice and Circle Healing

Mediation, restorative justice and circle healing for abusive teens and their parents may also be sources of help, but these methods are controversial. Transition house associations across Canada have warned justice officials that mediation and restorative justice can be destructive if the sessions are led by facilitators who do not understand the power dynamics of family violence, including parent abuse, and who do not accept that the victim is not responsible for the violence. The abuse must be acknowledged by all involved, and abusive teens have to be held accountable for their behaviour. The mediators or leaders must not undermine the parents in any way or treat the parents and teen as equals. The goal of the sessions should be the setting of ground rules that will help parents establish the necessary boundaries. There is a danger that in the alternative justice process, victims are left to find and carry out solutions, put safety plans in place, seek out community resources and make their own arrangements to access those resources. Youth, for instance, may be placed under house arrest, and it is their mothers who, without any training and little, if any, support, have to monitor them.

## Professional Responsibility

In spite of the difficulties parents have, involving professionally trained service providers is usually the best course of action. But in order to be effective in the long-term, professionals must acknowledge that they have a responsibility to take the complaints seriously and not to undermine the parents. In the courts, at the mental health clinics and with child welfare, parents are in a powerless position. Except in cases of child abuse or neglect, the service agencies' goal should be to help parents regain control of their families. It is important that everyone, including the police, doctors, ministers and other community leaders, be informed about parent abuse and understand the power imbalance that parents experience when dealing with service providers. Policies, guidelines and protocols to deal with parent abuse should be established by all services. Agencies cannot deal with this problem in isolation and should pool and coordinate their resources, rather than shuffling families from one agency to another as they do now. Much earlier intervention in parent abuse would save families a great deal of stress and service agencies a great deal of time and money.

## Counselling

In the long-term, counselling is one of the most helpful services parents can access to help them stop the abuse. Every Canadian, including children, adolescents and their parents, has the right to publicly funded professional mental health services, but public resources for counselling are scarce, and parents may have difficulty finding "free" resources in their area. The local shelter for battered women, women's centre, drug dependency service, children's hospital or child welfare service may have trained counsellors. If these agencies or organizations can't help, they may know of other places parents can try. When consulting professional service providers, it may be helpful for parents to keep in mind that professionals come from their own standpoint with their own preconceived notions: psychologists and psychiatrists usually see parent abuse from a mental illness perspective; police, probation officers and lawyers from a legal perspective; and social workers, counsellors and therapists from a family systems perspective. (The words "therapist" and "counsellor" are usually interchangeable, so for the purposes of this chapter, I refer to them as counsellors.) Understanding that service providers have different methods can help make the conflicting advice they receive less confusing to parents. But parents may also need an advocate as they work their way through this maze. It is important that the advocate works with the parents and doesn't take over and make them feel even more inept. They are already disempowered enough. Many people have negative experiences with counsellors, but a good counsellor can be an ally, so the choice of one is important. Parents may need to "shop around" to find a counsellor who is right for them.

One of the reasons parents sometimes have negative experiences with service providers can lie in the service provider's beliefs about parent abuse. In the 1995 study, most of the service providers interviewed said that they believed the problem of parent abuse begins with poor parenting practices and a lack of appropriate boundaries and limits. This is an overly simplistic and unsatisfactory explanation that pathogizes parent abuse and does not take into account the social context. It flows from the assumption that "the problem with kids" is their parents and that behaviour is an individual responsibility. When this is communicated to the parents, it leaves them feeling blamed and vulnerable at a time when they need support to feel strong and capable. It adds to parents' powerlessness when, as one mother said, "family therapists make you feel it's all your fault." Parents know they aren't functioning well as a family, and they don't need counsellors "to make us feel we weren't doing our job very well." Suggesting parenting classes is rarely a solution and is often demeaning and insulting. Most parents have successfully parented their other children and don't need to attend classes. Nor do they need to be told to establish boundaries. They know only too well that their efforts to establish boundaries are not working with this teen. They have simply run out of options. Eddie Gallagher says:

> Many parents I have dealt with have been to parenting classes, read parenting books and know what they should do with

reasonably cooperative children. They are often good at handling their other children and are emphatically not bad parents. Unfortunately many parenting courses and books assume a fair amount of cooperation from children and are very hard to apply to out-of-control children. Some otherwise good advice can make parents of such children feel worse. (2004: 7–8)

Service providers need to remind themselves that the chances are their clients are not being abused because they are weak and ineffectual, but rather they appear weak and ineffectual because they are being abused. Instead of being negatively labelled and blamed, parents need to be seen as a source of potential power to be tapped in finding a solution. Parents may have resources within themselves or their families that even they are not aware of.

It could be that service providers resort to blaming the parents because they themselves don't have any solutions. We do not yet fully understand what supports and therapies are effective, and it is a rare professional who feels he or she knows how to handle these cases. As a child welfare worker said to me, "We've missed the boat for a long time working with children who are showing signs of being abusive to their parents." Traditional counselling methods often do not work. Perhaps this is because parent abuse is not seen as a form of family violence and not recognized as an issue of power and control.

Blaming the victim is an unacceptable response to any form of family violence, even when the counsellor realizes that the perpetrators may have been victimized themselves and that the victims are not always innocent of harmful actions. It is no longer acceptable to think that a child may have deserved abuse at the hands of his or her parents or to blame women who are victims of spousal abuse. Equally, it is time for us to stop blaming the victims of parent abuse. A good place to start is seeing parent abuse as a form of family violence, although there are differences. There is a bond between parents and their children that is distinct from other bonds we form. In fact, caring about their children with all their hearts is often at the root of parents' inaction. Another difference is that, by law, these victims must care for the perpetrators of the abuse. This dilemma has to be acknowledged, and new strategies for handling parent abuse need to be explored.

An important issue for parents to explore is who gets the counselling: the abusive teen, the parents or the family together. Price believes that individual therapy with aggressive teens "is associated with notoriously poor outcomes" (personal communication 2001) and likens it to doing marriage counselling with one partner. But it may be helpful for the counsellor to see the teen alone for one or two sessions, although confidentiality is an issue. Some counsellors believe that in order to get the teen to confide in them, they have to promise to keep the teens' secrets. Others think that teens will talk about their lives whether confidentiality is promised or not and that keeping parents in the dark about their teen may be a form of collusion with the teen and contribute to further undermining the parents' authority. Some counsellors won't treat teens unless their parents are involved. It is interesting to note that, by law, counsellors are not always required to share with the parents any information from children. Getting teens to attend counselling sessions is not always easy. Even if parents can build rapport with a counsellor, sometimes their abusive children will not attend the therapy sessions. Again, parents need support with this. Jerome Price, in private correspondence with me (2001), said that he believes children are attempting to assert control when they refuse to participate in therapy. He suggests parents tell their children that they're expected to attend and there may be consequences if they refuse:

> In addition, if the child refuses to come, the parent tells their child that the parent is still going to the therapist and will talk about the child's fate with a stranger and make decisions about his or her life. These decisions will not be negotiable because the child didn't attend. Most children refuse to go with the expectation that therapy won't happen if they refuse to cooperate. The therapist must be skillful and directive enough to help the parents make changes whether the child cooperates or not. Most kids come when they realize the parent(s) are coming anyway because they want to keep control of the situation.

Eddie Gallagher persuaded one teen to attend counselling sessions by writing a letter to him, and this may be a strategy that parents could encourage counsellors to use. In his letter, Gallagher explained that he understood that teenage boys are often reluctant to attend counselling sessions and that the teen was embarrassed about his behaviour towards his mother. He wrote:

> This is good! The fact that you are embarrassed and ashamed shows that this is not the kind of person you want to be. I am quite

sure from talking to your mother that you do not want to grow up to be the kind of man who bullies people or abuses women. Your mother has told me that you are worried about being like your father. I assured your mother, and she said she had told you, that there is no gene for violence. (2004: 2)

Gallagher explained to the teen that most of the teens he counsels are "decent, caring kids." He outlined the dynamics that are often at play in parent abuse, including socially common misogynist (woman-hating) attitudes, the impact this has on women and the loss of respect towards women that often ensues. He also discussed the fact that many parents try hard to be perfect. He left the teen to decide which, if any of these dynamics, applied to him and assured the teen that he could control his abusive behaviour. He asked the boy's mother to leave the letter with her son and not wait to see if he read it, because the teen might tear up the letter without reading it if he had an audience but may not be able to resist reading it in private.

In some cases, counselling the parents without the teen is recommended. This could be the case when the parents are having marital difficulties and making the situation worse by quarrelling or siding with the child against each other. However, when the presenting problem is parent abuse, the couple's marital difficulties should not be allowed to side-track the main issue. When parents have done all they can, they may need to be counselled without the teen to help them accept that there is nothing more they can do to control their child.

Another important question is how long counselling should last. Some counsellors believe the road to health is very long and may take years, while others say that most therapy is accomplished in a few sessions. Price (2002) says you haven't tried it until you have tried it for three months. Parents need to know the counsellor is willing to hang in there with them, through the ups and downs, through their failures to act and the failures of their attempts.

## Social Learning Theory and Stress Theory

Before choosing a counsellor, it may help for parents to understand that counsellors, psychologists and psychiatrists are trained to understand what causes certain behaviours, based on a number of theories (Rybski 1998). In working with families who are experiencing parent abuse, two of the theories they rely on are social learning theory and stress theory. A familiarity with these theories may help parents understand the questions that counsellors ask and the changes they propose.

Social learning theory suggests that children are not born aggressive and violent; they learn how to react to situations by observing the world around them. This is the most common theory used to explain parent abuse and can be parent-blaming. Although teens learn from other adults, their peers and the media, counsellors generally assume that teens learn from their parents who gets rewarded for what behaviours and what behaviours are acceptable. If children see their fathers getting their own way by being abusive to their mothers, or their mothers being able to rule the roost with manipulating or harsh or unpredictable behaviour, children may indeed grow up to believe that these are successful and acceptable strategies. They may also learn to minimize these forms of behaviour and to blame the victim.

This process does not usually occur consciously. Teens are often not mature enough to make logical, impartial decisions about their behaviour or the impact of that behaviour on others. They simply repeat behaviours they have observed or experienced, from their parents and others, and attempt to control others with manipulation and/or aggression. They also learn that control exercised through violence is situation-specific, that is, people don't behave the same way towards everyone. The father who abuses his wife may well not treat his friends or his boss the same way. Social learning theory may explain why teens who witness their fathers abusing their mothers may also abuse her. The teens have learned that this person can be victimized and controlled by force. Of course, not all teens respond the same way. Some may observe the consequences of the abuse and repeat the behaviour of the victim by becoming depressed or passive. Others, even after years of observing violent patterns of behaviour, may reject violence for themselves.

Stress theory is also commonly used to explain parent abuse. This theory explains violent behaviour by suggesting that it is the individual's reaction to stress. For teens, stress can be a single, major event like a car accident or their parents' separation, or it can be an event that may appear more trivial to others, like losing something or being treated disrespectfully. But for many teens, everyday living is stressful. The fact that many teens find school an ongoing stress was discussed earlier. Stress can even be caused by positive change, like getting a new job or moving to a new home. The resources and strengths the individual has at the time of the event usually determine how they handle stress. Everyone, including teens, needs to understand that life is a series of "bumps," and we all need to learn how to keep our balance, or at least regain it. If teens have not learned coping skills or are without sufficient emotional, physical or financial support, they may be unable to handle even a relatively small amount of stress. Again, this is where some parent-blaming can surface. Service providers generally believe that if teens have a good relationship with their parents and if they observe their parents' good relationship with each other, they learn positive coping skills. If the parents are what psychologists call "deficient" in coping skills and their relationship with their child is either disengaged or overly enmeshed, and if there are no other strong, positive influences in the teen's life (such as a grandparent or teacher) these skills are not acquired. Without positive coping skills, teens' self-esteem may drop. They often become depressed or angry, and they act out their feelings impetuously. This adds to an already stressful situation and the stress spirals. Some teens and adults use drugs and alcohol in response to stress and this often compounds the problem. How stress is perceived also influences how it is managed. Some people manage stress well simply because they believe they are strong and they can cope. For others, being stressed can heighten the stress of a situation. When a teen's inability to cope is thought to be at the root of the abuse, people tend to excuse the behaviour. They say things like, "He's so angry," or "She has such a hard time at school."

## Directive and Non-directive Counselling

It may also be helpful for parents to have some understanding of two of the basic counselling styles they are likely to encounter: directive and non-directive. It is totally acceptable for a client to ask the counsellor which style they use. Directive counsellors believe they are the experts and their job is to devise solutions and direct the parents. Counsellors who practise this style believe that counselling fails when parents do not have sufficient faith in the counsellor to follow directions and try out the suggestions. These counsellors believe that hopelessness or some other form of emotional resistance is blocking opportunities for change and that their task is to instill hope and help the parents break free of despair, in spite of the violence and destruction of their families. Directive counsellors do not allow people to say there's nothing they can do. The counsellor recognizes that, in the absence of new ideas, parents have resorted to old patterns of parenting, unsuccessful as they may be. In Price's words, "The goal is for counsellors to be choreographers or quarterbacks who call the plays to help parents take charge of their families" (Price and Cottrell 2002). The counsellors act as a "parent" to the "child" the parent has become. They are the experts with the skills and training to take the initiative, devise new strategies for the family and instruct the parents to carry them out, even when the parents are doubtful they will be successful. They do not expect the parents to find their own solutions to the problem. As Price puts it, "If you take your car to the garage, you wouldn't have faith in a mechanic who asked you how to fix it." While there is no doubt that this method has been used with success, directive counsellors should keep in mind that seeing the client as a "child' may breed opportunities for counsellors to exercise their power over a client and in doing so block the empowerment of the parents.[1]

The medical model used by most psychiatrists and psychologists is a form of directive counselling. These professionals generally believe that the problem is individual and rooted in the personalities and mental ill health of the teen and/or the parents, and that it requires a diagnosis and treatment from a person with a mental health education and authority. As was discussed in Chapter Nine, the major criticism of the medical model is that it can be fatalistic and pathologize/medicalize the problem and often shifts the power away from the parents without addressing the abuse.

Client-centred, or humanist, counselling, in contrast, is less directive. Here I discuss one particular form of humanist counselling, feminist counselling, because the analysis of family violence as a matter of power and control is at the basis of this method. Feminist counsellors believe that personal problems are often created by social oppressions, such as poverty and racism, and that it is society, more than individuals, that requires changing. Hence the slogan: the personal is political. Feminist counsellors have faith that women, even though they may appear damaged, have demonstrated their ability to be strong and courageous by seeking a counsellor to help them. They also believe that woman are trained to take care of others before themselves, even at their own expense, and that they tend to blame themselves for everything that goes wrong in the family. Accepting the woman where she is and accepting her truth rather than trying to impose their interpretation of the woman's life, trying not to contribute to society's "mother blaming" and instead helping clients understand what it is to be "good enough" as a mother are all parts of this counselling method. Believing that the woman will make the right decisions for herself when she can and inviting women to look at their decisions and analyze why they are making those decisions, feminist counsellors support their clients in finding their own voices. They act, in the words of psychologist Beate Blasius, as "midwives," supporting the parents in "giving birth" to their strong, capable selves.[2] Rather than focusing on the teen's abusive behaviour, feminist counsellors acknowledge that many women feel compassion and protectiveness towards their children and identify with their children's pain and that parents are in a double-bind: they can either deal with the problem — usually by calling the police or requesting the child leave the home — and feel guilty and upset, or they can do nothing and continue to be abused. Taking action is extremely difficult. Unlike directive counsellors, the feminist counsellor is not in "rescue mode" but instead helps clients to find their own solutions while acknowledging that not all people are ready to act. The counsellor probes to find out what the client perceives the problem to be, what they have done to solve the problem, what they have and haven't tried, and why. When that information is identified, the counsellor helps the client explore her choices. This requires the counsellor to listen for clues to where the client is coming from. It is a slow process and requires patience.

Whatever method is used, the counselling must be grounded in the understanding that the natural hierarchy of the family is for parents to have authority over their children. Teenagers are not adults, they are dependents, and when parents are being abused there is an imbalance of the natural hierarchy. Abused parents are not parenting. The tail, as Jerome Price says, is wagging the dog, and, because they are afraid, angry and despairing, the abused parents sometimes react like teenagers themselves. They revert to the child within. This is not unusual. We all do it, or have done it in the past, when we are upset or feel helpless. The counsellor's task is to help the parents be aware of what dynamics reduce them from their potential as competent parents, so they can make a conscious decision about when they will act like adults and when they can let their feelings show. Parents need help not just in establishing boundaries but in feeling more secure about what they are doing. The counsellors can also help parents assess what is happening in their families and encourage them to use their own wisdom in calmly assessing how violent their child is, which behaviours they can safely ignore and which they should deal with.

## Collaborative Relationships

The relationship between a counsellor and an abused parent has to be collaborative, or it isn't helpful. The reason why the abuse is continuing is a problem for the parents and counsellor to solve together. The counsellor can help identify the reason and help find a solution, but there are no overall techniques that can be used with every family. The dynamics in each family must be assessed individually. The counsellor's task is to help parents identify what is causing their inability to parent this child, explore how they feel and why they do the things they do, and support them in making necessary changes. In order to grow, we all need to understand our feelings and how we function, but most of us cannot do this alone. When parents trust the counsellor as an ally, when they understand the process and feel supported and capable enough, and when both have a shared goal, they will devise good solutions to their problems and can change their lives. If parents hesitate, the counsellor must be able to hear what is causing this. Parents will reject a proposal if they do not feel they have a say in it or if they feel it won't work for them.

Counsellors need to show what Omer (2000) calls "therapeutic respect," that is, the counsellor must believe the parent and not undermine them. They must respect the parents' pain, values and achievements and acknowledge that the parents suffer the abuse and the fears that go with it, because their children are important to them. For parents to begin to cope with abuse, these feelings have to be acknowledged. When a counsellor does this and does it with empathy and compassion, it sends a clear message that the parents are important people worthy of someone else's time and care. The counsellor shows the parents how their failure to act entrenches the abuse and adds to their fear and how this fear in turn makes them less able to act.

Asking parents to name their worst fear is a good way to begin the road to ending the abuse. Exploring why they aren't ready is part of the process. For instance, instead of telling the client to call the police when they are afraid for their safety, the counsellor explores why the client has not called the police. It is not unusual to find that a client blames herself for her child's abusive behaviour and feels, for this reason, it would be "unfair" to get the child into trouble with the law. This self-blaming may be because in the past the child has been exposed to, or been the victim of, abuse. At this point, the client's guilt needs to be worked with. When parents think the abuse is a "phase" that will pass, it may be an indication that they feel calling the police is a step that would mean they are giving up hope, that will take the situation to another level from which there will be no going back. Parents may be so emotionally attached to the child they don't want to do anything that will harm or sever that connection, and they need support to see that their inaction is allowing the abuse to continue or even worsen. Above all, clients need to be understood and believed. Therapy will fail if the counsellor doubts the client or is, in the words of Price, "too eager to change people and too slow to understand them" (1996: 6).

## Conclusion

In the end, parents have to consider themselves the managers of the situation and not depend on anyone else to do it for them. As this parent wisely put it:

> *I think we're going to have to be very watchful and assertive to get whatever help is available. It doesn't just come to you. A lot depends on what you reach out for. You have to be a discernible person to be able to access what's out there. You can fall through the cracks pretty easily.*

Parents have to work, and it can be practically a full-time job, to ensure they and their families don't fall between the cracks. It means making endless phone calls and personal visits; it may mean telling service providers that they won't take no for an answer. A friend can be a support person to vent to about the frustrations and someone to go along on visits to school teachers, psychiatrists and lawyers. Keeping a record of the teen's behaviours, moods and encounters with the legal and mental health system and of medications, dosages and clinical appointments is a good practice and will confirm that the parent isn't exaggerating or crazy. A record of conversations with school officials, specialists and so one, as well as names, dates and telephone numbers can help to keep the chaos organized. Above all, parents should remind themselves that professionals are working for them, and while respecting their position and expertise, don't always assume they know best. The parent's inner voice is the best guide, and in the end, the decision always rests with the parents (Mason and Kreger 1998). There are also a number of things parents can do without professional help, or to augment the help they are receiving, and this topic is explored in the next chapter.

## Notes

1. Private correspondence with Catherine Hennigar-Shuh and Nancy Gray. The following section on feminist couselling is based on discussions with thse wise and skillful therapists.
2. Private correspondence, April 2003.

# 11. The Ultimate Goal
## Regaining Control and Healing the Relationship

*What a beautiful day it is here today.*

Parents want safe, healthy and loving relationships with their happy and well-adjusted teenagers. They desperately care about their families and know only too well that they need to ensure the safety of their families. But there are no prescriptive guidelines for parenting an abusive teenager, and the parenting methods they use for their non–abusive children are not working with this one. They live with the abuse because they don't know how to stop it. Sometimes, as hard as it is, there is nothing more parents can do to help their teen. They need to accept that they have done their best and emotionally and physically protect themselves. Lori said:

> I remember saying to the guidance counsellor at the school last year that I felt like I was the only one that could save him. She said that maybe I can't. I think I'm finally at the point of knowing that. I've done everything that I can do for him. I've taken him to his appointments and I've worked with the school and tried to talk to him and now there is nothing else I can do for him. That scares me.

With understanding and support, parents can make healthy decisions about their lives and act on those decisions to begin the long and difficult process of ending the abuse. And the chances are that the abuse will eventually end. Of the thirty-four families we spoke with in our first research project, the abuse had ended in sixteen.

## Making Changes

There are no easy solutions, but there are changes parents can make that may help. Actively trying to end the abuse instead of being immobilized can give parents strength, can help them feel better about themselves and, when the abuse is over, can help them live with themselves more easily knowing they tried to find a solution. As stated earlier, it is often precisely when parents attempt to restrain teens and impose boundaries that the violence erupts, but parents who manage to set clear limits and consequences can reduce the abuse. When youth are forced to accept the consequences of their behaviour, the rewards of violence may be minimized and the secret exposed.

Setting limits and stopping abuse can be a complex process, requiring different forms of interventions for different children, depending on the individual situation of each family. Counsellors and others in the helping professions do not all have the same beliefs and styles. Parents may have to try a variety of approaches to find out what works for them. Even though abused parents are already exhausted, and "shopping around" takes time and energy, doing this work allows them to shift their time and energy in a positive direction and to break established patterns that are not working for them.

## Self-care

The first step on the road to ending the abuse is self-care. Self-care begins with changing the focus from the teen's needs to the parents' needs — the need not to be victimized, the need to recognize that the abuse is neither acceptable nor "normal" and the need to have loving, gentle and firm control of their children. Once parents are more present for themselves, they can become more aware of the dynamics at play, not just of their own feelings and responses, but those of their teens and the professionals they encounter. By focusing on their own needs, parents can begin to emotionally separate from their teen and not let guilt and anxiety overwhelm them. An essential ingredient in self-care is being gentle with themselves and accepting that shock, relief, anger, depression, sorrow and a sense of failure and loss are normal feelings. Parents who are abused have had their self-confidence eroded and are devastated. Their confidence is further eroded because the abuse seriously impacts on their work life. Indeed, it is remarkable that many parents are strong enough to function as competent, self-assured people at work and in the rest of their lives. That's how the secret is kept. These are not weak people. They have just lost their parenting grip and need to regain their inner strength, so they can feel secure and self-confident everywhere, including in their homes.

Exercise, meditation and talking to a supportive listener can help build this sense of self-worth. That in turn helps parents consciously decide where they want to focus their energy and strengthens their ability to cope with the situation. Even little things like taking a warm bath by candlelight or pouring their feelings into a journal can help. One mother said that what worked for her was when she put the feelings aside and went out with friends. If she refused to allow herself to think about her problems for a short time, she could enjoy herself. She had to make an effort to do this. But when on occasional evenings, she gave her mind a rest and had fun with her friends, she found she returned home refreshed and had more energy to deal with her son.

## Learning about Parent Abuse

The next step is for parents to learn about parent abuse. What they already know is that the standard parenting techniques they have used with their other children, or seen other parents use, are not working with this teen. Reading about parent abuse helps them to recognize that what they are experiencing is abuse and that they aren't the only parents experiencing it. This breaks through the isolation they are feeling. One mother said she read the parent abuse report and "found it quite amazing to read because it was describing accurately what was happening to me and I hadn't seen that described anywhere else." Another said that reading about parent abuse helped her realize she was being abused, that she was normal and wasn't going crazy. "For a while," she said, "I thought I was going nuts." It also gives parents hope when they see that they can look for help. Not all parents find the answers in reading. One father told me, "No amount of reading helps. Nothing helps. It's hell." But it does help parents understand their rights and make better-informed decisions.

Once they are clear about what they can do, they are less afraid to seek help. For instance, when they understand what the police can and cannot do, they are more likely to call them. Learning the facts about drugs and alcohol use and its consequences can help reduce the fear parents experience. If the teen is using drugs or alcohol, making changes may not be possible until the substance use is addressed. Information is available at adolescent drug treatment centres. Parents may find it useful to contact a centre for advice, rather than try to deal with the teen's problem themselves. Familiarizing themselves with resources available in their community will help them make wise choices. A call to the local library is a good place to start the search for this information. There are also many websites parents may find helpful, although most do not directly deal with parent abuse. Many libraries have computers available for public use free of charge, and staff are often willing to give a quick "how-to" to patrons who do not know how to use the computers. See the Appendix for details of helpful websites. Also lists of hundreds of websites can be found by typing "parenting teenagers," "parenting adolescents" and "parent abuse" into the search function.

Reading about parent abuse with the teen can be a preventive step. Teens don't always realize their behaviour is abusive, and when they see it in print, it can be a wake-up call for them. One mother sat down and read through the parent abuse booklet (which was discussed in the introduction to this book) with her daughter. She said that together, using the categories and descriptions in the booklet, they went through the girl's behaviours and named them. The teen was able to see that her behaviour was abusive, and together they looked for a group that would help her.

## Talking about the Abuse

Once they are fully informed, finding a safe place to talk about their experiences can have a profound impact on parents. Just talking can help break the isolation and reinforce the naming of what is happening. It also helps parents see more clearly the dynamics in their families and the need to take action and change the relationship. One mother said it was only when she started talking about her attempts to reach her daughter that she realized she had been letting her daughter "call the shots." Because parent abuse is not generally recognized in society, parents need to be ready for the negative reactions they may encounter when they talk about their troubles and stand firm in their resolve to be in control and not be "guilted." As one of my friends says, "Don't take guilt trips. Take a trip to the mall, to the next county, to a foreign country, but not to where the guilt is." Beware though that the shame and guilt mothers experience is often reinforced by people who hold the parent responsible for the teens' behaviour. They may think they know the solution and get annoyed when the parent refuses to do it their way. Because of this, parents may want to find a professional service provider who understands the dynamics of parent abuse, and this is discussed in the next chapter. Parents may also want to join an internet chat group such as <http://forums.talkcity.com/TC-Parenting_Te/chat>.

## Exploring Ourselves

Before they access professional help, parents may want to explore their feelings about the abuse on their own. One of the techniques that people find helpful is to write a letter describing the pain the teen has caused them. Although the letter is written to the teen, it is for the eyes of the writer only and never sent. Written without censorship or editing, the letter includes all the worst thoughts and fears the writer has. The act of writing can help parents move from a jumbled mass of emotions and to sort out their feelings. A second letter could detail what it is the parent wants from the child: a wish list of all the teen could possibly do and give to the parent. This helps the parent identify what it is they want.

Through this process of reading, talking and writing, self-awareness can develop, and parents may see that their own response to their teen's abuse has been negative or even abusive, and, if they have a partner, they can see whether not working together has been a contributing factor. While it is not always easy in the face of aggression and may take a supreme effort, using more positive communication strategies and establishing firm boundaries and rules with appropriate consequences for the entire family may help to end the abuse. When everyone in the family takes anger and sarcasm out of their voice and treats others with respect, the teens often respond positively by role-modelling their family's more respectful communication. This may lead to them feeling more valued, so they stop using violence to gain a sense of personal power and safety. It can also lead to increased intimacy with their parents. Teens who abuse don't feel close to their parents. It's cyclical: when teens feel a connection with their parents, they are more likely to get the positive attention they need and less likely to abuse.

## Being Present in Teens' Lives

Another change parents can make is to have more presence in their teen's life. We have already discussed the fact that from when they are born, children begin to separate. They have their own distinct personalities, and before they even learn to walk they are expressing their needs and desires. As this process evolves, parents allow more and more freedom for the child, until, by the time they are teenagers, parents are allowing the teen to make many of their own decisions and have time away from them. This is the last step before they leave the parents' home and live independently. The separation is not an ever-increasing straight line. Parents allow little children to walk and talk without help, but when the children are endangering themselves, they step in. When their little children move too close to a hot stove, or start using foul language, or do any of the other self-destructive things children can do, parents know they have to pull in the reins. I sometimes allow my six-year-old grandson to cross the road without holding my hand, but as soon as he starts to run or I see he isn't paying enough attention, I take him in hand again, even though he protests he can do it on his own. I will keep giving him chances, and keep taking his hand, until I see that he is old enough to know how to cross the road independently. We do that with all aspects of our children's lives when they are young: what they wear, who their friends are, where they go. Eventually, by the time they are teenagers, we have let them go on most things. We allow them to make many of their own decisions and to go out without us. But when they are engaging in destructive behaviour towards themselves, their parents or others, it is time to take them in hand. It is time for more, in the words of Omer (2000), "parental presence." The "time in" as opposed to the "time out" method.

Parents who are truly present in their teen's life are sending the clear message that they care, that the teen is important enough to warrant the parents not spending that time with friends or at work or watching television, important enough to want to know where the teen is and who the teen is with. Teens want to feel self-confident and powerful, they want to feel special. When they are acting out, when they choose violence as a means to an end, it is because they are searching for something that is missing in their lives and crying out for guidance. When parents are present, when they are actively engaged in their teens' lives, the teens see that the parents have a commitment to be there and are really concerned that the teens are safe and out of trouble.

Teens hide their need for their parents' presence and will, of course, protest when the reins are tightened. They will protest even more when their parents start having more contact with others, such as the parents of the teen's friends, teachers, principals and guidance counsellors, doctors, church leaders, police and probation officers. But uniting with other people who are in the teen's life can give parents more strength and control, and it sends a message to the teen that their parents are not alone in the struggle. Arranging a suicide watch of friends and family can be especially helpful if the teen is threatening to hurt themselves or to commit suicide. Communication with the school is essential, even when parents feel unsupported by the staff. When parents know how well their teen is progressing at school, follow the teen's homework and know the teachers, the teachers will see that the family is involved and concerned and will be less likely to see the parents as the cause of the problem. If the teen is also acting out at school, the principal is less likely to simply expel them. Teens will say that their parents don't have the right to "interfere" and are too controlling. These teens are wrong. Parents have the right to have a presence in their child's life and to stay in close communication with the people who are a part of it. The teen soon learns that their privacy is a privilege earned by responsible behaviour. Once they understand that their abusive behaviour is costing them their privacy, they may decide to improve their behaviour to regain it.

## Acting, Not Reacting

Parental presence does not mean talking at the teen. Endless talking, complaining and begging usually fall on "deaf ears" and do more damage than they repair because they are a substitute for action. Less talk, more action is an effective strategy. Most parents don't act; they react to the their teen's aggression. It is important to remember that the actor in any situation is in control. Recognizing who is acting and who is reacting in any situation is key to ending the abuse. Only when parents see that they are reacting, can they begin to stop it. To do this, parents must examine whether they are encouraging the escalation of the abuse by occasionally giving in, against their better judgment, to the teen's abusive demands. A typical scenario is when parents say no to their teen, the child threatens and the parents give in. This encourages the violence because each time the interaction becomes more intense. Parent abuse is usually an interactive process that tends to increase in intensity with time; the teen acts and the parents react ever more intensely. Ending the abuse requires a non-reactive, non-violent approach. If parents do not react, but say no and calmly stick to it, they will regain power.

So how do parents avoid reacting? The first step is to identify what Price (1996) calls "reactivity hot buttons." That means identifying when the abuse starts, when the teen is pushing or pulling, and when the parents are pushing or pulling in response. For example, many teens exert power by refusing to speak or by using foul language they know will upset their parents. This "pushes the parents' buttons" and, in an attempt to force the child to communicate or to stop the swearing, the parents react, often with empty threats or with screaming in frustration, actions that only make the situation worse.

Price offers the following plan for action. After an altercation, parents need to think calmly (and calm is the operative word here) about the situation and recognize when their feelings are interfering with their common sense. In a healthy, balanced relationship, parents act and the teen reacts, parents define and the teen accepts or challenges those definitions. The person who defines the meaning and the one who influences the other's feelings is in control, so a first step is for parents to define the meaning of each event and identify who succeeds in getting the other to feel guilty, frightened or doubting themselves. The next step is to have a plan in place for how to deal with the next challenge, and this includes realistic consequences. The aim is for parents to give consequences that cause the teen to modify their behaviour. When tempers have cooled, perhaps hours or even days later, parents can share the plan with the teen. Power is gained when parents do not automatically and immediately share what they know with their teens. They do not need to spell out consequences to the teen and, in fact, can apply consequences in ways that are unpredictable to the teen but well-planned and thought out by the parent. Control is also gained when parents challenge locked doors, secret phone calls and any other suspicious behaviour. Abusive teens have not earned the right to privacy. It is also not important that the children agree with the parents' method of intervention. They will, of course, balk at any attempts to restrict their freedom and are more likely to object to controls than willingly go along with them. What is vital is that the parents communicate the clear message that they are in control. The consequences may include simple things like taking away the use of the car, phone or computer, or taking away designer clothes the parents have paid for.

But many abused parents have already taken these actions, and after a while the teens respond with, "Go ahead and see if I care." As Theresa said, "[H]ow many times can you punish someone?" Her son did not respond to threats to take away his television privileges or to stop him seeing his friends and "waving around a large wooden spoon and threatening to use it had absolutely no effect." Some teens seem impervious to any form of conduct control. And so the parents must move in closer and take the more serious steps of contacting or going to the school daily or calling the police. It is often the teens who threaten to call the police or child protection authorities, and a powerful tactic parents can use is to call the teen's bluff and tell them to go ahead.

If parents know when they usually react, the next time the teen is pushing or pulling, they can choose to do little or nothing at the moment of abuse. Instead, they can activate their plan, unless, of course, someone is going to get hurt and then they are left with no choice but to act. For instance, Omer suggested to two parents that when their "grounded" son tries to leave the house to go, for instance, to a dance, instead of reacting by yelling and physically stopping him, they let him go. As soon as the teen has left the home, the parents call the support system they have put in place, and together the band of adults go to the dance. He predicted that within a short space of time, the teen would leave the dance and return home. People may think this is a nasty ploy and it is unacceptable for parents to embarrass their teens, but if this action averts abuse, perhaps, in this case, it is the lesser of two evils and the ends justify the means. The teen is unlikely to verbally and physically abuse his parents in front of others, whereas, if they had tried to stop him at home, the situation would have probably turned aggressive.

## Learning Respect

If adequate steps are taken early enough, teens can learn to stop being abusive, to take responsibility for their actions and not blame others, and to recognize that feeling angry is acceptable but acting violently is not and that acting out aggression is not healthy or constructive. In other words, they can learn to respect themselves and others. Peter Monk, the social worker I referred to earlier, asked teens what helped them stop abusing their parents. One teen said it was learning to think before he acted and learning how to respect himself and others, "and not always have to overpower people" (1997: 110).

Before they are willing to begin this learning, teens must first recognize that their behaviour is abusive. Simply talking to an adult other than their parents, such as a family friend, church member or professional counsellor, can help them see their behaviour more clearly. When teens are able to make meaningful connections with community members, the violence is sometimes reduced, partly because, through this connection, teens begin to recognize and expand on positive aspects of themselves and attempt to honour the values of others with whom they are connected. Parents should monitor who their teen is talking to and make sure the person isn't colluding with the teen. Teens, like men who abuse their intimate partners, usually deny or minimize their behaviour, and they justify whatever they have done by convincing themselves that they were provoked into violence. An adult outside the family can help them understand that even if they think they didn't really hurt their parents, or their parents are exaggerating, and no matter what is done to them, violence and aggression are inappropriate responses. One of the first places parents can look for such support for their teen is the local intervention program for abusive men. Libraries usually have contact numbers for these organizations. The teen's friends can be a good source of support too. Having a friend name the behaviour as abusive can be a wake-up call.

Teens who have been victims of abuse are often angry and full of despair, and once they recognize that they have been harmed and need to look after themselves, they are better able to develop a non-violent lifestyle. Again, this often entails seeking, or being willing to accept, support from others. With this support, they can begin to process their personal issues, and this can reduce the rage and anger they feel about what happened to them. They learn that nothing can erase the past, but they can live with it, as did this teen who told Monk, "the memory will always be there ... I have to learn to let go" (1997: 110). Whether they have been abused or not, abusive teens can learn to identify and express their feelings more appropriately. When they are better able to ask for what they want instead of resorting to violence, they can learn to sidestep or prevent conflict from happening. As this teen says:

> I just know that I don't want to do that today. Because I can get my freedom and I can get my power and control or whatever in other ways. I know that I can talk to people, that I can communicate now. I can talk about things and feel my feelings. (Monk 1997: 110)

Learning to empathize with others is a crucial component of change and helps teens take responsibility for their behaviour. Once they learn how to feel the pain they are inflicting, they have a deeper understanding of the emotional consequences of their behaviour and are more likely to feel remorse and change their behaviour. Even for teens who know precisely what they have done and are ashamed, admitting it is not easy. They may express remorse in ways other than words, as this wise mother saw:

> I think his actions speak louder than words. He's never been a person to apologize for anything, to say, "I'm sorry." So I think in some of the ways, some of the things that he does around the house, I think he's trying to ... apologize. (Monk 1997: 127)

Monk believes that when youth are encouraged to focus on future goals and dreams, they are less likely to be violent. For example, he noticed that young women he talked to were more likely to modify their violent behaviour if they were pregnant or even just thinking of having their own children, because they want to stop intergenerational patterns of abuse. One young woman told him she was pregnant and "sort of grew up more" (1997: 111). Another said:

> I feel like if I don't get help right now I don't know what the hell is going to happen with my kids, right? Because I know ... I'm going to have kids and I don't want to be doing that to my kids. (Monk 1997: 111)

## Non-punitive Approaches

Monk's research and his experience as a social worker have led him to the conclusion that change is more likely to occur when parents use non-punitive approaches. We want our teens to behave decently, not because they are threatened, restricted and punished, but out of genuine compassion and concern for others. We set curfews for our teens, for example, because we want to know where they are and that they are safe. But curfews are threats that restrict the teen's exercise of their own power. A more powerful tool than setting curfews may be to explain to the teen that we want them to stay in contact so we know they are safe.

When parents role-model positive communication, the teens begin to feel valued and are less likely to be violent. Sometimes this is because the teens no longer think they have to be violent in order to get attention or to feel a sense of personal power. They don't feel rage anymore because their needs are getting met. They feel they belong and are loved and don't have all that anger. More positive communication also offers the opportunity for increased intimacy between teens and parents. Teens are less likely to assault those they have a connection with, and so the development of intimacy between the parents and their teens helps to reduce the abuse. It is not easy to do, but focusing on the teen's positive characteristics can help. A social worker told Monk about a teen he worked with who was abusing his mother:

> [W]e had these wonderful conversations about seeing his gift of compassion, and his tenderness, and realizing that it came from his mom, and his culture, and his traditions. And he was able to identify those gifts, and to really hold them and cherish them. [And] as long as we were able to maintain this kind of conversation and this kind of life ... the violence within the home vanished. (Monk 1997: 152)

However, until they are self-reflective, teens are likely to accept the culturally dominant message that it is acceptable to act powerful by being rude, and they will make excuses for their abusive behaviour. Empty and dismissive responses are nothing more than their attempts to avoid responsibility. Common "lies our children tell us," as one social worker calls these, are:

- Everybody does it.
- It's not like you haven't done it before.
- I'll never do it again.
- It's all your fault.
- It's my friends.
- Can I go now? Are you finished?
- It's my life. I can do what I want.
- I'm sorry.
- You don't trust me.
- I won't lie to you.

Getting promises in writing can help, and parents may want to have the child sign a written list of rules such as this one:

I agree to do the following:
- Attend and fully engage in school.
- Keep parents informed about where I am.
- Do chores (e.g. clean up my room)

In our house we will always treat each other with respect. This means no physical or verbal abuse. These things are forbidden in our house:

Name calling
Hitting or hurting others in any way
Damaging other people's property
Making threats to hurt myself or anyone else
Stealing or borrowing things without permission
Playing mind games
Insisting others buy things they can't afford

Signed: _____

Date: _____

Parents should choose the consequences appropriate for each rule violation and ensure that they have support in place to help them stay in control to carry through with enforcing them.

## When Teens Leave the Home

Sometimes, in spite of all the parents' efforts, the situation remains out of their control, and the abuse ends only when the parents separate themselves from the teen. Even a temporary separation can be beneficial. A few hours can make a difference. Parents are often emotionally torn about this, but recognize their need for separation. Once Lori and her husband took separate vacations so they could get away from their son. Lori said:

> It sounds horrible and sad, but we have to get peace of mind from somewhere. I just want a day that I don't have to talk about Christopher, worry about Christopher, talk to the police about him, talk to the school. I just want to go out, get groceries, go shopping and have a day that I have peace of mind, a normal day.

Irene found the separation from her son invaluable:

> I put a lifetime into taking care of him. I did not have a lot of support as I was isolated and could not bring friends to my house because his behaviour was so erratic and he made the house such a mess. He used my isolation as weapon. The six weeks he was away was a big new discovery for me. During this time I have strengthened my bond with friends and started to develop a social life.

One mother refused to let her son into the house after an abusive outburst, and he spent the night sleeping on the street. The next day he returned contrite, and there has been no further abuse. But allowing a young person to sleep on the streets is a frightening thought for most parents. The teens are very vulnerable "out there" and can easily be harmed or get into trouble:

> It's been a couple of weeks now, he's resourceful, but he has to eat and sleep somewhere. I'm not scared he'll be found frozen dead somewhere, but he's involved with criminals. He's either going to be the victim or the perpetrator of a serious crime. The phone doesn't ring without an adrenaline surge. Having him in jail had some advantages: I knew where he was.

One mother described her intense anxiety: "I was a basket case the first time she took off.... I had neighbours looking for her. I wasn't sleeping or eating. She could have been dead in a ditch." This mother was the sole financial support in her family, and she couldn't afford to jeopardize her job by losing nights of sleep waiting with dread for a call from the police. It was the anxiety she experienced when her child left that made her realize she had to act. "When I finally knew the only relief I'd get is if the police called and said she was dead, I knew it was time to cut the ties. I was hoping God would relieve the pain."

Respite care in the form of short-term supervision of the teen by someone other than the parent can give parents a break from the stress of the situation. It is a means of escaping the immediate threat of abuse and can send a strong message to the teen that their behaviour is not acceptable. Sending the teen to live with a relative or friend for a short period may help, but this is not always a good solution because it can undermine the parents' authority, especially when the relative or friend is not as careful a guardian or does not watch the child as closely and impose rules and sanctions the same way the parents do.

Social services occasionally find group or foster homes for the teens, but as we saw earlier, they admit they have few places to put abusive teens, and group homes are not always a helpful option. Unfortunately, removal of the teen on a more permanent basis may be the only solution for ending the abuse. Refusing to allow their teens to live at home gives parents the time and space to begin dealing with the long-term issues associated with the abuse. However, long-term solutions are difficult to find and throwing a child out of the home can be a very painful experience. This mother describes the horror:

> I took the house keys away from her. It was all cold and calm. I took her by the arm to the door. It was cold, dark and I passed her her coat and put her out. I couldn't believe I'd done it. I didn't cry. It was like I was in shock. Then I was worried and afraid because I hadn't checked with her father. I realized it was because I was in so much pain. I was like an animal with a foot in the trap. It was like gnawing off the foot to relieve the pain. I didn't know how much longer I could go before I killed her or ended up in the mental institute. I just couldn't stand it anymore.

Theresa's son left the home after years of abuse. Since then he has been involved in abusive relationships with young women which resulted in two separate changes of assault and issuing death threats. When he contacts her now, Theresa feels "strong enough to put the phone down or throw him out of the house," but she says, "Without a doubt he is still abusive." In spite of this, and much to her family's concern, she cannot cut him out of her life altogether and still bails him out financially and with food.

When a teen has left the home, it may be a relief. One mother told us, "It has been so much more peaceful since Jane left, even my cat's purring and cuddling up to me now." But there is often a sense of loss. Siblings no longer have their brother or sister, and parents grieve for the loss of their child and for the family as a unit. This experience is especially traumatic in single-parent families where the teen is an only child. When the teenager is removed from the home, parents lose their child, and in some families, they also lose contact with grandchildren as well. One mother travelled a thousand miles to see her daughter when she heard she was pregnant:

*I was excited but guarded. I was afraid I'd start to love her again and she'd hurt me again. I was afraid I'd love the little one and she'd use her against me. When the baby was seven months old we had a fight on the phone and she threatened I wouldn't be allowed to see the baby. I can't allow myself to be as close to the baby now.*

Sometimes the teen's attitude improves after a while away from home and they may want to return. Decision-making at this time should not be made out of the parents' feelings of guilt. It is important that the parents think through what they want so that they can retain their new-found control. To avoid the abuse starting again, parents need to be very clear about the rules and the consequences for breaking the rules.

## Conclusion

To deal with the long-term issues associated with the abuse, parents need time and space in order to begin taking control of their lives, to assert their right for safety and the safety of their other children and, if possible, to start to heal the relationship with the abusive teen. Healing and relationship-building can only continue at a pace the parents are comfortable with as they work through the anger and come to a place of acceptance.

# 12. Spreading the Word

We all have a responsibility to be informed about parent abuse and to help end it. Parents shouldn't have to do this work alone, especially parents who are screaming for help. But how do we get everyone on board, especially as the issue of parent abuse is rarely discussed in public?

Educating the public to recognize and name abuse is a start. But whose responsibility is it to do the educating? At the time parents are experiencing abuse they are in crisis. Community awareness is not their primary concern, and they rarely have the time, energy or desire to organize public information sessions. Even after moving beyond the crisis, parents may not wish to talk publicly about their experiences. There are others of us though, such as friends, family, service providers and other professionals, who can spread the word and promote awareness.[1]

## Distributing Parent Abuse Materials

One way to educate the public is the distribution of materials about parent abuse. Those published by Health Canada are available free of charge and details about how to obtain them are in the Chapter Two endnote. Counselling services may well appreciate having the documents on hand to read and to give to clients. One counsellor told us that she found the Health Canada materials very useful:

> I ordered it for a client in victim services who had gone to the police with a complaint against her daughter for physical assault.... I liked that we were encouraged to photocopy it and distribute it to others. My colleagues were intrigued. This was fabulous for people in child welfare. I have been passing it on to clients as a front-line worker and with other people working in the same area.

Although distributing material may seem simple enough, it requires a fair amount of organization. Linking with an established agency may help as it confers legitimacy on a project, and the organizations' resources, such as a meeting space, contact information, etc. would be available. The organization you approach could be one that has an interest in the topic or one with which you are involved for some other reason. Police victim services departments, single-parent, family and community centres, and counselling services, such as the family service associations, are places that may be interested in working on this project with you.

Once that link is made, the first step is to consider forming a project group or committee. Even for a single task, a committee is useful because when people share tasks, the project can be more manageable, and even fun. In addition, good ideas are often generated. Friends, colleagues and others in your area may be interested in helping with the project.

If you do decide to gather a group, the success or failure of the project may depend on how well people understand the goals of the project and how much they feel useful members of the group. The goals of this project, for example, might be to gather materials about parent abuse and to distribute the materials locally.

The first meeting could be a description of parent abuse and the presentation of two or three clearly thought out project goals. It is always advisable to involve those at the meeting by asking for their input and ideas. People feel a part of the group if they are actively involved and can draw on their experience, rather than being passive listeners. When all group members feel included and have a sense of "ownership," energy is generated and the group becomes more dynamic. Participants should be asked if they agree with the goals or have any suggestions for changes. Respect for group participants is essential. It is important to acknowledge everyone's input, thank them for it and allow it to be discussed. Nothing is gained by someone going away feeling unheard or dismissed.

The next step is to develop an action plan based on the project goals. The plan helps make clear what is going to be done, when and by whom. Information about where you can go to access information about local resources needs to be gathered. A good question to ask is: Where do we access information? Where in our community do we find out information? The list could include libraries and community, family resource and single-parent centres. Contact information for these places, such as telephone numbers, should be collected. Once this is done, the places could be telephoned to find out if they are willing to display the materials you collect. A possible introduction could be:

> Hello, my name is ———. I am working with (name of organiza-
> tion.) We are concerned that parents who are abused by their
> children have access to information about this topic. We would
> like to know if you are willing to display the booklet.

If they are willing, it is a good idea to ask for the name of a person
you could telephone to let them know when you will be arriving with
the materials. Whether this organization is willing to display the material
or not, you may want to ask if they have suggestions for other places in
the community that you could approach.

One person in the group should take the responsibility for checking
that materials have been ordered, received and distributed as promised.

## Working with Schools and Community Groups

Another possible venue for public education is schools. Most schools are
now actively engaged in anti-violence work, and teachers are often
receptive to suggestions for school projects. If they have the information,
high school teachers may be willing to address the issue of parent abuse
in the classroom. Teachers may be interested in an in-service session too.

Parents may also want to offer to talk to groups and organizations in
the community such as churches, parent resource centres and women's
shelters. Lists of these places can usually be found in the telephone
directory and at the local library. Speakers are usually invited to speak for
about an hour, and, with ten minutes for introductions and thanks, a
well-planned twenty-minute talk with twenty minutes for a question
period works well and allows the speaker to run overtime if needed.

## Organizing Workshops

Organizing a workshop could help to bring the issue out into the open.
In Nova Scotia, the response to a number of one-day workshops on
parent abuse has been encouraging. In one rural area, the RCMP Volunteer Community Assistance Service joined with the local branch of the
Canadian Mental Health Association and hosted a one-day workshop on
parent abuse. Organizers were amazed to have over one hundred and
thirty people request to attend. The participants paid $25 each, and that
covered the costs, including a lunch. Almost every participant felt the
day had been extremely worthwhile and the evaluations were overwhelmingly in support of the endeavour. A workshop is useful if every

service provider can take away just one idea that alters their practice, and every parent feels less isolated. After one workshop, a service provider said:

> I learned a lot from a parent abuse workshop I attended. It made me realize that I've been seeing teenagers in isolation. Now I see them as part of a family, and I am much more sympathetic and helpful towards the parents.

## Organizing Committee

Workshops take careful organization and can be extremely time consuming so forming an organizing committee helps to share the work. It also brings together people with a variety of skills and knowledge about the topic and the community. Soliciting the support of an existing organization or a group, or even better, asking an established agency to sponsor the event, has many advantages, not least of all that it gives legitimacy to the work. People are more likely to trust and respond to an invitation to attend an event that is sponsored by the Family Service Association than one sponsored by an individual they have never heard of. The committee should include service providers who have experience working with parents, such as police officers, social workers, therapists, community health nurses and legal aid workers. These people have a vested interest in learning more about how parent abuse affects their work and could help design and organize the workshop, as well as publicize it in their workplaces and communities. It is also important that parents who have experienced abuse are part of the group as their experience will influence the content of the workshop. Often, when people begin to pool their experiences, they find that collectively they have a great deal of knowledge about the topic that they didn't realize they had.

The work of the committee is to make sure that all bases are covered. This group will make the decisions regarding the workshop content, format, participation and practical things such as location.

## Workshop Goal

The first thing to discuss is your goal: What do you want to achieve? Why are you organizing the workshop? To raise awareness? To provide information and supports to parents? To provide information to service providers so they can better support parents?

As there are no quick fixes for the abuse parents are enduring, it is important to have an attainable goal. While simply raising awareness may not seem all that significant, it is an achievable goal that may help parents know they are not alone and can be a starting point for them to name what is going on and move forward. It could also result in altered professional practices and more responsive services for parents.

What the workshop cannot do in one short session is to be a therapy session for parents. Other parents or professionals may not be equipped to provide support or counselling and trying to help one distressed parent can derail the entire workshop.

A handout sheet with suggested goals can be found in Appendix Two.

## Participants

The question of who the workshop is for — parents, service providers or the general public — will depend on what your goals are. Although service providers can also be abused parents, you may want to plan separate workshops for these two groups, because the focus will be different.

The number of participants is also a consideration. This may depend on the size of the room available. I have conducted workshops for as few as twenty participants and as many as a hundred. Changing locations after the publicity has gone out can create chaos, so it is advisable to limit registration to the number you can accommodate.

## Workshop Content

It is important for the organizing committee to be clear about the workshop content. Is it specifically about parent abuse, or are you trying to link it to other issues that are high on the current public and government agendas, such as bullying? Will the workshop cover a wide variety of aspects of the issue, or is it more specifically about such things as community supports? The content will be slightly different for parents than for service providers, but you may want to discuss the same issues with both groups, e.g., what parent abuse is, who is doing it and to whom, and what strategies parents find helpful.

The length of the workshop — an hour or two, half a day, a full day, or two days — will influence how much content can be covered. It must also be decided precisely when the workshop will be held and whether it will be on a weekday, an evening or a weekend.

Most successful workshops have a mixture of learning approaches: presentations, brainstorming, large group question and answer periods, and small group discussions. By providing variety in the workshop, the participants stay more energized. It may be helpful to let participants discuss why they think the abuse is happening and strategies for stopping the abuse, such as where they go for help and their experiences with both friends and family and professional service providers.

## Presentations

Parents and service providers have much to learn from each other, and representatives from each group could be invited to make presentations. Parents have a tremendous amount of experience, and all participants can learn how the issue affects individuals when parents speak. Having two parents speak reinforces the fact that parents come from a wide variety of backgrounds but share common feelings of despair and a common, often more frustrating than fruitful, struggle to find professional support. Participants may find it helpful to hear from parents about their experiences of feeling blamed and how counterproductive guilt is. Other parents can find it reassuring that they aren't alone in this experience, and service providers can learn what it is that parents need and aren't getting. If no parents are willing to talk publicly about their experience, perhaps someone could give a summary of some of the stories in this book.

Similarly, both parents and professionals can benefit from hearing from service providers, such as police officers and counsellors, about the service they offer and the difficulties and barriers they face in supporting parents. Presentations can be on panels or with individual presenters. To keep the listeners' attention, panels should never have more than three or four presenters, and each should speak for no more than ten minutes. After the speakers have presented, participants should be given time to ask questions. Again, ten minutes of questions is usually sufficient to keep the group engaged. A good moderator or facilitator for the panel presentations and questions will keep things moving.

Public speaking is difficult for most people, so speakers should be instructed in detail on what is expected of them and how long they have to speak.

## Large Group Discussions

A discussion that involves all the workshop participants as one large group can be dynamic and informative. To begin a discussion, a simple question should be asked, such as, Why do teens abuse their parents? Or Where can parents go for help? If the question is too complicated, participants may have difficulty understanding what they are being asked to respond to. Large group discussions require a skilled facilitator who will make sure as many people as time allows get a chance to speak and no one "hogs the floor." It is also essential to stop the discussion at the allotted time, or it will take time away from the next planned session or force the workshop to run overtime, something that most participants detest.

## Small Group Discussions

In small group discussions, it is recommended that, to keep the group focused, only one topic is given for discussion at a time. The topic should be written on a flip chart or handout, and the workshop facilitator should make clear ahead of time precisely how much time they have for the discussion.

People have a great deal of knowledge and experience, and group discussions provide the opportunity for them to bring that knowledge to the fore and to share it. It is therefore important that the atmosphere is not threatening or intimidating in any way. When they share their experiences with others, most groups of parents will arrive at the conclusions outlined in this book: it is impossible to profile an abused parent or an abusive teen; the causes are complex and multitude; and the solutions difficult to come by. They also share tips about what works for them and reinforce and encourage each other. When a woman who feels crazy, alone and terrified, hears another mother say, "Sometimes I feel like I'm going crazy," or "I feel so isolated," or "I'm so scared because I can't get any help," it can be a tremendous relief. When a counsellor who is discouraged because parents always end up feeling blamed and threatened hears another counsellor ask, "What are we doing that makes parents feel so blamed?" it can be a breakthrough. These may be words they have been too afraid to ever say before. Once the feelings are shared, solutions can be discussed.

One person in each group should be named as the group facilitator. Sometimes it is helpful for workshop organizers to identify in advance a facilitator for each group. This person's task is to make sure that all group members are given equal speaking time and that the group remains respectful and safe. If a group member attacks another or interrupts, the facilitator can gently remedy the situation with statements like, "Perhaps we should try not to judge each other," or remind participants that they should give each other time to finish.

## Location

Libraries, community centres and even grocery stores may have a room they allow community-based organizations to use, often for a very small fee or even free of charge. The room should be easily accessible, especially for parents who do not have their own cars. Adequate, affordable parking is another consideration. We found that seating participants at tables of six made organizing group discussions easier, and this influenced our choice of room. If lunch is not provided on site, it is important to locate the workshop near low-cost restaurants that will serve reasonably quickly.

## Publicity

Brainstorming how to get the word out about the workshop could begin with the organizers thinking about how they learn about things in their community.

A poster advertising the workshop can be designed and distributed to local notice boards. Don't forget to phone ahead and ask permission! A prototype for a poster can be found in Appendix Two. Churches, family and parent centres, shopping centres, community and women's centres and community health clinics may welcome such notices.

The best advertising is an article in a local paper or an item on television, and a call to the editor or producer will often achieve this. A media release can also be mailed or faxed to media outlets, including radio and television stations and newspaper offices. A frequent response to media releases is a request for an interview. One or two of the organizing committee members should be identified as the people who speak to the media and their names should be on the media release. If possible, at least one person should be someone who has experience talking to the media. Much more is said in interviews than actually gets published or aired, and once the words are spoken, you have no control over how they are used, so be prepared to hear one short statement taken out of context and broadcast to the community! A wise rule is take a reasonable, thoughtful approach and never make negative or condemning statements without giving them a lot of thought first and making sure your facts are correct. Our media release produced a request for a television reporter to attend the workshop with his camera. We decided not to permit this, as we felt it would inhibit participants and stop them from speaking freely at the workshop. Instead, at the workshop we announced that the television station was interested and invited participants to call if they were willing to "go public" with their stories. Notices can also be sent to local television cable stations for inclusion on their public service announcement (PSA) notice boards. Posters, PSAs and media releases should include the five Ws: What the topic of the workshop is, where and when it is taking place, who is invited, and why (the goal of the workshop). It is important to make clear on the publicity whether lunch is included in the workshop fee.

## Food and Drink

Having coffee, tea and juice available is a must at workshops. People often feel more relaxed with a drink in their hands, and beverage breaks allow participants informal time to chat with others. However, the cost of the beverages must be factored into the workshop fee. Less time is needed for a lunch break if it is provided on site, but again, the cost is an issue. Most people are satisfied with a bowl of soup and a sandwich, with perhaps fruit for dessert, and this can be an economical meal. If you want to keep the cost of the workshop low, participants can be "on their own" for lunch, but if you do this, be warned: participants sometimes get caught up in their lives and don't return to the workshop, or return late.

## Handouts

It is often helpful for the participants to begin the day with two handouts: the goals of the workshop and a workshop outline. Suggestions for handouts can be found in Appendix Two. The facilitator and others involved in the workshop may require workshop outlines with more details, such as the names of the presenters.

## A Facilitator

Your choice of facilitator could make the difference between a successful and a not-so-great workshop. The facilitator keeps the workshop on course and moves it along. It is easy for participants to get sidetracked and off the topic, to go into too much detail, to speak too long or to become overwhelmed with their own issues. A good facilitator will help keep the participants focused. There is a delicate balance between pursuing interesting digressions and allowing too much rambling. A good facilitator knows the difference.

It is the facilitator's job to introduce participants to each other. Most people like to know who else is in the room. With twenty or fewer participants, the facilitator can invite each participant in turn to stand and introduce themselves. Clear instructions should be given. Parents could be invited to give their first name and the ages of their children. Service providers could be instructed: "Please stand and introduce yourself, giving your name, where you work and what you do, and anything else about yourself you would like us to know. Let's start at the back with John." When facilitating a panel or presentation, the facilitator introduces each speaker so that the participants know who they are listening to. The introduction includes the person's name and job title, for example, "Our next speaker is Constable John Smith. Cst. Smith has worked with the Halifax Police Youth Division for ten years and has a great deal of experience responding to calls from parents who are being abused." The facilitator should cut the speaker off after the given time allowance. Presenters can be so enthusiastic about their topic that they forget how long they have been speaking and have been known to take time that was allotted to others.

It is important that people's fears and anger are acknowledged, but organizers should be mindful of what they are trying to achieve. Instead of allowing the workshop to deteriorate into a professional-bashing session, for example, the facilitator could acknowledge that most service providers want to help and often do an excellent job. While it is important to acknowledge the hurt participants have experienced, try to keep the workshop more positive by requesting helpful suggestions for how parents have coped and where support has been found.

Above all, a good facilitator must understand the topic, and while being compassionate, not get swayed into joining in on anything destructive.

## Supports

Parent abuse is a very sensitive, loaded topic, and parents who are in crisis often need support. It is strongly recommended that if the workshop is for parents, one or two counsellors are identified for them to talk to in case the content of the workshop triggers feelings in them that they have difficulty getting under control. It is also recommended that boxes of tissues be made available at the beginning of the workshop. It can be explained that crying is allowed and participants should feel free to ask for support but will not be "rescued" without their request. That way, they will not be afraid to let their feelings show and will know help is there but it will not be imposed on them.

At the beginning of the workshop, parents should also be cautioned that there is no such thing as confidentiality in a group setting and they should be careful about how much they choose to share with strangers. Participants may have also suffered abuse from their partner, or have experienced abuse as a child, and emotions about these events may come up at the workshop. Parents should be reminded that they must be careful not to share something because they feel safe that they will regret later.

## Evaluations

Evaluations are a very useful tool for organizers to understand what did and did not work for the participants. Evaluation sheets should be kept short and simple. They should never be more than one page long, and the fewer questions with more room for the participants to write their thoughts, the better. A sample evaluation sheet can be found in Appendix Two.

## Forming a Support Group

Organizing teen or parent support groups requires hard work, skill, experience and funds. Parents who try to get support groups going for parents and for teens often find it difficult and fraught with problems. As this mother explained: "It's so hard. We need a facilitator, an outreach worker to work with us and get it established so people who work and are dealing with the problem don't have to take it on."

Before embarking on this venture, it is strongly recommended that you contact your local support group centre. These centres are skilled in helping with the set-up of support and self-help groups. You may be able to find the phone number and address for the organization near you at this website: <http://www.mentalhelp.net/selfhelp>. Local organizations such as churches and community and women's centres may also have staff with the necessary time and skill who are interested in getting involved.

## Note

1.  This chapter is based on my own experience and on discussions with Linda Roberts, a community developer who has spent a great deal of time spreading the word about issues of interest. I am indebted to Linda for her willingness to share her skills, experiences and wisdom.

# Conclusion
## Help Wanted

In the end, *When Teens Abuse Their Parents* leaves us with many questions. But it does give us a sense of the dynamics in families where the teens are controlling their parents and the natural family hierarchy is turned upside down, and what happens when parents turn to the helping professions for support in regaining leadership in their families. We don't even know how many families are in this state of disorder or if more teens abuse now than in the past, but we do have evidence that parent abuse is widespread in Canada today. The good news is that parent abuse is beginning to come "out of the closet." Researchers are paying more attention to the issue, and parents are no longer keeping silent. They are naming the abuse and begging for the help they need and deserve.

For far too long, parents have been keeping their secret from relatives, friends and co-workers because they don't trust that they will be understood. They suspect, and are often right, that the first reaction will be to blame them for the abuse they are suffering. This blame is internalized and, hopeless and helpless, parents blame themselves and feel like failures. Tremendous courage is required for parents to speak out, because we, the general public, and that includes the helping professions, are not ready yet to stop individualizing the problem and stop looking for where the parents have "gone wrong."

Admitting to themselves and others that their child's behaviour is abusive is also extremely difficult. It was despair about the lack of loving compassion in their families and their desperation to find a solution that drove parents to talk to us. They had sought help but to little avail, and they felt alone with their pain. Our research was also seen by these parents as an opportunity to reach out and help others who are equally isolated.

Their stories confirm that there is no typical abused parent nor typical abusive teen. Abused parents can be comfortably off financially or struggling on inadequate incomes, homemakers or with jobs in the workplace, single parents and those with partners. Despair was their commonality. The teens also have a wide range of experiences: some had been abused or had witnessed their mothers being abused, some used drugs or alcohol, some did well at school, some were diagnosed with mental illnesses. What teens seem to have in common is that they abuse to control their parents.

Parenting today in a world of globalization and rapid social change can be extremely stressful. Teens have more freedom and a greater sense of entitlement than ever before. They are aware that they have rights but sometimes forget that they also have responsibilities. Canadians struggle to be good parents in a society that offers little support or understanding when teens misbehave. Like all parents, parents who are abused have made mistakes. They have been too severe with their children or overly permissive, and often inconsistent. In many families, it is only one child who is abusive, which makes it difficult for parents to figure out what kind of parenting the abusive child needs. Spending quality time with their teen is a constant struggle, in part because any time with the teen is fractious and in part because teens aren't expected to spend time with their parents. Having any control over their teen's lives is a battle because teens feel they are entitled to their freedom and that parents shouldn't interfere in their lives.

Finding the causes of parent abuse, in my opinion, may be an interesting academic exercise, but it doesn't help families in trouble. There are so many complex webs of causal possibilities, and poor parenting is only one possible part. Teens are affected not only by family dynamics and their own individual personalities, but also by social dynamics. Social values, sexism, racism, classism, ability and religion all play a part. And these are not necessarily causes. At best we can say they are dynamics that may contribute to abuse. This is the reason that we should stop blaming already stressed and struggling parents. Blame does nothing more than exacerbate the problem. But blame them we do. In addition, we add to the burden by giving them sole responsibility for stopping the abuse. Ultimately, the fact is that, whatever the "cause" and even in extreme cases of serious mental illness, teens' abuse of their parents is unacceptable.

Parents are not only held solely responsible for finding the cause of the abuse, they are also left to find the cure and to care for their teens while they are being abused. Most abused parents try "the whole gamut" of support services and devote years of their lives waiting for appointments and attending them. But, in the words of one parent, "nothing works," and not finding the help they need, they are left with an increased sense of isolation, shame and futility.

There are, however, some things parents can do. Parents can begin to take control of their lives, to assert their right for safety and the safety of their other children, and, eventually, they may be able to start to heal the relationship with the abusive teen. Healing and relationship-building can only begin, though, if parents gain the support they need. They can think of themselves as the "managers" of the situation and be assertive in asking for the help they need. Professionals are working for the parents, and parents have the right to respect for their opinions.

Perhaps, also, what parents need are support groups run by professionals, because, when parents can talk openly about their experiences, when they have information about the dynamics of abuse and when they really believe that they have the right and duty to keep themselves and their families safe, they are in a better position to stop the abuse. This is especially so in the early stages. If this service were available to them, they would have more support and courage to take the steps that would lead them to regain their leadership in their families. When the abuse is full-blown, this kind of support is even more vital.

Above all, these parents and their families need everyone's respect and support so they can build the self-confidence needed to regain leadership in their families. How much more helpful it would be if, instead of condemning the parents, we all did our part in raising the next generation, and we did it with compassion and understanding.

# Appendix One

## Websites

<http://www.teamcares.org/Teen_Abuse.htm>
TEAMCares is an organization devoted to helping victims of family violence, including parents who are abused by their teens. Their site opens with a full page outline of the report I wrote for Health Canada and links to a number of informative sites. One of the most interesting services they offer is a book called *How To Take Advantage Of Your Parents* by John LaDeux. For $5 parents can order the book on line, and/ or they can order a hard copy to be sent to their teen. LaDeux writes:

"If you are the victim of abuse by your children, my heart goes out to you. I too was the victim of abuse by my children. This book has been written to the Abuser but it is also a good tool to use to inform yourself of the possible methods of abuse that can and are probably being used on you. By knowing what possibly can happen, will help you to overcome the abuse and put an end to it. The main thing I want you to remember is, 'Do not let your children destroy you. It is not your fault that the abuse is happening. You are not alone. There are millions of parents that are victims of abuse by their children.' Seek help as soon as possible by telling someone that can help. Your neighbor, friend, doctor, family lawyer, pastor or priest. The sooner you tell someone, the sooner you will be free of the abuse.

"I know that it is difficult to report abuse by your children. It is embarrassing and frightening at the same time. But believe me, it is far better to do so than to be destroyed by someone who apparently doesn't care what happens to you even if it is your own child. Perhaps the child needs psychiatric help and doesn't know it or doesn't want to admit it. In any case, what they are doing is wrong and it has to stop.

"What can happen to you, the victim, is far worse than what can happen to the abuser. The abuser will receive help in what ever form is necessary. You on the other hand may be destroyed completely if the abuse isn't stopped. My wife and I had endured abuse by our children over a period of 5 years. In our 38 years of marriage, I had never heard my wife talk about suicide until the time of the abuse.

"The first thing that happens is that you 'want' to help the child. You will do everything in your power to help the child straighten out their life. After several months of being taken advantage of, you realize that this situation may never end. Your life is disrupted as well as your financial security. As the abuse gets worse, depression sets in."

LaDeux lists the symptoms of depression then continues: "If you have these symptoms, then you must do something about your situation immediately. Don't put it off, hoping that the situation will go away on its own. It won't. It will only get worse. You don't deserve being abused. You wouldn't do it to someone else, don't let it continue to happen to you. The quickest way to put an end to the abuse is to take a stand. First you must let the abuser know that you know what they are doing. The abuser will deny it and rightly so. Maybe they do not realize what they are doing. Nevertheless; it is time they did realize what they are doing.

"Then tell others, friends, neighbors, doctors, lawyers, pastor or priest about the situation. By talking about it to others, your abuser(s) will be exposed for what they are doing. It is called, "bringing it out into the light." Will they get in trouble? There is an excellent possibility that they will. For your own good, let the chips fall where they will. It has come to a point that it is either you or your abuser. If you can't do it on your own, then get a friend or someone you trust, to stand by you for support.

"There are two ways to use this book. First, read it yourself to learn how abuse will come and what techniques they will use on you. Secondly, give the book to the child personally. By doing so, they will become aware that you know what they are doing and that in itself may be enough to stop the abuse. If you are afraid to do that, send it to them in a brown envelope with no return address. The shock of other people knowing what they are doing may be enough to bring them to their senses.

"The book is written solely to the abusers. It is 'raw' in nature and content. It has been designed to fit in with their frame of mind. It is also written in mentor form to give the appearance of the abuser being instructed by another abuser.

"In conclusion, stay strong and fight the battle to the end. The end being your freedom, once again, to live the only life you have on this earth. It is your life. It is precious. Don't let your abuser steal if from you without a fight.

"As for your abuser. Their life is their own. How they live it and what they do with it, is their concern as long as it doesn't take from someone else's life. Your concern should be first, protecting your life. Then helping your child in whatever way possible without destroying yourself. You cannot help them if you are not around to do so. You can only do so much. You have done it. Now help them by allowing them to get the help that they really need."

<http://www.parentsoup.com>
Parent Soup has won many awards, including the America On Line (AOL) Member's Choice Nomination, where it was cited as one of the four best websites for families, and a 5-Star Rating for being "an excellent online resource" from Netguide, an internet guide. The site states: "If you are the parent of a teen, get ready to deal with everything from driving to sex! Ready or not, the teen years can often be rocky. Fortunately, they are also amazing and rewarding too." Parents can choose to browse a variety of pages, including "What to do about stealing," "Learn more about raising teens" and "Parenting Issues Debate." The site also includes a discussion room where parents can post notices and talk to one another. The postings have titles that include:
>    Need SERIOUS help with 15 yo son
>    Out of school suspension
>    Please help, heartbroken dad
>    Need some support
>    Help — I found a boy in her bed!
>    More drinking with 15 yr old

<http://www.instituteforattachment.org>
The Institute for Attachment is a licensed, non-profit, internationally recognized treatment, training and child placement agency in Colorado. According to their website, they have successfully treated hundreds of children with attachment disorder since their inception in 1972. Their Mission Statement says: "We are committed to transforming the lives of children with attachment, behavioral and emotional disorders and their families, and promoting healthy family relationships."

The institute provides treatment for families and children with attachment, behavioural and emotional disorders, along with the following services; advocate for supportive, responsive communities; research

effective treatment methods; educate about causes, effects and prevention of attachment, behavioural and emotional disorders; nurture and
empower families; and train professionals in the assessment and treatment of families and children with attachment, behavioral and emotional
disorders.

The website includes interesting information about attachment disorders that parents may find helpful. The Institute also has an extensive
publications list and offers courses and counselling, but there is a charge
for these.

<http://www.ggoss.com/parentpg.htm>
On this website, parents can post questions for Dr. Goss, who, so the
website states, answers them all. Although I was unable to find any
information about Dr. Goss and recommend that parents use their own
judgment about any advice they are given or information they glean
from the site, the site is certainly chock full of links and information. The
site includes advertisements for books Dr. Goss has written, and the first
chapter of the books is on the site and can be read for free.

According to Dr. Goss: "Parenting is a BIG subject. There are a lot
of Online resources available pertaining to specific issues. My own area
of interest centres around child and adolescent behavior. I believe that
there's a lot of mis-information being spread around, with the result that
many parents are feeling confused and powerless to manage their children, while kids and teens as a group are tending to be less responsible
and harder to control. I have been providing parent education seminars
for nearly twenty years and have learned that *well-educated parents* have no
trouble at all raising good kids in a conflict-free home atmosphere."

<http://www.mifamilytherapy.com>
This is the site for Jerome Price's Michigan Family Institute and contains
information about a new publication package by Jerry Price and his
colleague, Judith Margerum, *The Right to Be The Grown-Up: Helping
Parents Be Parents to Their Difficult Teens*. This parenting skills training
program is primarily for therapists and contains practical strategies for
working with parents whose children's behaviour is out of control.

# Appendix Two

Workshop Handouts and Poster

## Parent Abuse Workshop

### Goals

- To raise awareness about parent abuse

- To learn to recognize parent abuse

- To identify practical resources and community supports for parents and their teens

Workshop Poster

# PARENT ABUSE WORKSHOP

Are your teenage children...
yelling at you?
hitting you?
threatening to hurt you?
calling you names?
stealing your money or possessions?

Who is the workshop for?
Parents who are experiencing abuse

When is it?          Thursday, March 22, 2004
from 9:00 – 11:30 am

Where is it?         Captain William Spry Community Centre
10 Kidston Road, Halifax

Cost?                This workshop is free, but there are limited spaces. Registration is required

How do I register?   Call the Community Centre at 479-4487

Parent Abuse is any act of a child which is intended to cause physical, psychological or financial damage to gain power and control over a parent.

What is the workshop about?
The workshop will explore research on the issue and parents' experiences

Many parents initially deny that their child could be abusive towards them. When they accept the behaviour is abusive, they often feel guilty, isolated and unsupported. Parents fear for their safety and that of their family. At the same time, they fear for the welfare of their abusive teen.

This Workshop is sponsored by:

# Workshop Outline

9:00 a.m.     Registration
              Participants are given an outline of the workshop and a copy of free materials.

9:30          Welcome and Introductions
              Workshop organizers and support counsellors are introduced, and housekeeping items, including location of toilets and telephones, are announced. The workshop leader briefly outlines the plan for the day, and discusses workshop ethics, including respect for others, allowing others to speak and not judging or interrupting.

10:00         Panel Presentation
              A parent and two therapists each give ten-minute talks and answer questions.

10:30         Break
              Participants have the opportunity to chat informally and get to know each other.

11:00         Small Group Discussion
              Participants are invited to discuss the following questions: Is the abuse of parents by their teenage children an issue in our community? Is there more violence towards parents now than in the past? Why is this happening? After the small group discussions, brief reports are shared.

Noon:         Lunch

1:00 p.m.     Panel Presentation
              Representatives from local counselling agencies, the women's shelter and the police give ten-minute talks about their experiences with the issue and answer questions.

2:00          Small Group Discussion
              Participants are invited to discuss the following questions: Why don't people talk about this issue? How can we make it a public issue? After the small group discussions, brief reports are shared. Participants are urged not to make a suggestion for action unless they are willing to take the lead. A skit dramatizing a variety of forms of parent abuse and the effects on parents is performed by a parents' group.

4:00          Closure
              Participants are invited to share one thing they will take away from the day.

# Workshop Questions to Stimulate Discussion

- What is parent abuse and who are the perpetrators and the victims?
- Who is most at risk (mothers, fathers, single parents) and why?
- Does abuse by boys and girls differ in form or frequency?
- At what age does the abuse start?
- What forms does the violence take?
- What causes the abuse?
- Is there a connection between parent abuse and other forms of abuse?
- Has the teen witnessed violence in the family?
- Is there a link between parent abuse and other forms of violence in our society?
- How do families cope?
- Where do parents and teens turn for help?
- What kind of help do they receive?
- What strategies have victimized parents found helpful?
- What resources and tools do parents and counsellors need?
- How can the abuse be prevented or lessened?
- What responsibility is taken by professionals?
- What are the attitudes of professionals towards this issue?
- Who is addressing the issue?
- How can the issue be better addressed?

# Evaluation Sheet

What did you find most useful about this workshop?

_____

_____

_____

_____

_____

What did you find least useful? What could have been done better?

_____

_____

_____

_____

_____

We may use your comments to help us organize future workshops on this issue. Do you have any suggestions for us?

_____

_____

_____

_____

_____

Please write here any further comments you would like to share with the organizing committee.

_____

_____

_____

_____

_____

# Afterword

This book primarily explores the experiences of mainstream Canadians because, to date, that has been the focus of research and writing on parent abuse. However, I do understand that immigrant, African Canadian and First Nations parents face additional challenges. They also have many positive parenting practices that mainstream Canadians can learn from. In an attempt to begin to fill this gap, Justice Canada has funded research that has enabled my colleague and friend, Dr. Madine VanderPlaat, a sociologist at St. Mary's University in Halifax, Nova Scotia, to work with me to explore parent abuse in immigrant families. We are currently collecting information from parents and service providers that will enhance our understanding of the added challenges immigrant parents face and that, we hope, will improve our ability to support those who are experiencing abuse.

My sincere thanks to the team of people who are so generously steering this research: Annemarie van Vuren; Mohamed Yaffa, Family Violence and Cultural Awareness Program, Metropolitan Immigrant Settlement Association; Diane Crocker and Evie Tastsoglou, Department of Sociology and Criminology, St. Mary's University; Jeff Karabanow and Wanda Thomas Bernard, Maritime School of Social Work, Dalhousie University; Judy Crump, Nova Scotia Department of Justice Policing and Victims Services; Karima Bashra, Nuru-Hadi Translation Services; Najma Sharif, Department of Economics, St. Mary's University; Nancy Gray, Director, New Start Men's Intervention Program; and Verona Singer, Coordinator, Halifax Police Victims Services.

# References

Agnew, R. 1992. "Foundation for a general strain theory of crime and delinquency." *Criminology* 30: 47–87.

Agnew, R., and S. Huguley. 1989. "Adolescent violence toward parents." *Journal of Marriage and the Family* 51: 699–711.

Alibhai-Brown, Yasmin. 2003. "Parents Under Fire." *Community Care*, November 20–26.

Ambert, Anne-Marie. 1992. *The Effect of Children on Parents.* New York: Hayworth Press.

Arrigo, M.J. 1982. "Battered parents in California: Ignored victims of domestic violence." *San Diego Law Review* 19: 781–800.

Artz, Sibylle. 1998. *Sex, Power and the Violent School Girl.* Toronto: Trifolium Books.

Bandura, A. 1973. *Aggression: A Social Learning Analysis.* Englewood Cliffs, NJ: Prentice-Hall.

Bass, Ellen, and Laura Davis. 1988. *The Courage to Heal: A Guide for Women Survivors of Child Sexual Abuse.* New York: Harper Collins.

Brezina, T. 1999. "Teenage violence toward parents as an adaptation of family strain." *Youth and Society* 30: 416–444.

Browne, K.D., and C.E. Hamilton. 1998. "Physical violence between young adults and their parents: Associations with a history of child maltreatment." *Journal of Family Violence* 13: 59–79.

Caplan, P.J. 1989. "Take the blame off mother." *Psychology Today* October: 70.

Carlson, B.E. 1990. "Adolescent observers of marital violence." *Journal of Family Violence* 1: 285–299.

Cazenave, N.A., A. Murray, and M.A. Straus. 1979. "Race, class, network embeddedness and family violence: A search for potential support systems." *Journal of Comparative Family Studies* 10: 281–300.

Charles, A.V. 1986. "Physically abused parents." *Journal of Family Violence* 1: 343–355.

Cornell, C.P., and R.J. Gelles. 1982. "Adolescent-to-parent violence." *The Urban Social Change Review* 15: 8–14.

Côté, J.E., and A.L. Allahar. 1994. *Generation on Hold: Coming of Age in the Late Twentieth Century.* Toronto: Stoddart.

Cottrell, Barbara. 2001. *Parent Abuse: The abuse of parents by their teenage children.* Health Canada, Ottawa.

_____. 2002. "Help Wanted: The abuse of parents by their teenage children." *Systhema* 3: 212–224.

Cottrell, Barbara, and Peter Monk. 2004. "Adolescent-to-parent abuse: An overview of common themes." *Journal of Family Issues* 21,6.

Coupland, Douglas. 1991. *Generation X.* New York: St. Martin's Press.

Dauvergne, Mia, and Holly Johnson. 2001. *Children Witnessing Family Violence.* Ottawa: Canadian Centre for Justice Statistics.

Dekeseredy, Walter S. 1993. *Four Variations of Family Violence: A Review of Sociological Research.* Ottawa: Health Canada.

Dornbusch, S., J. Carlsmith, S. Bushwall, P. Ritter, H. Leiderman, A. Hastorf, and R. Gross. 1985. "Single parents, extended households, and the control of adolescents." *Child Development* 56: 326–341.

Eccles, Jacqueline S., and Bonnie L. Barber. 1999. "Student council, volunteering, basketball, or marching band: What kind of extracurricular involvement matters?" *Journal of Adolescent Research* 14: 10–43.

Eckstein, Nancy J. 2002. *Adolescent-to-Parent Abuse: A communicative analysis of conflict processes present in verbal, physical, or emotional abuse of parents.* University of Nebraska, Lincoln, USA.

Edleson, J.L. 1999. "Children's witnessing of adult domestic violence." *Journal of Interpersonal Violence* 14: 839–870.

Enang, Josephine. 2000. "Mothering at the Margins." *Canadian Women's Health Network* 4, 2: 7–8.

Evans, E.D., and L. Warren-Sohlberg. 1988. "A pattern of analysis of adolescent abusive behavior towards parents." *Journal of Adolescent Research* 3: 201–216.

Frizzell, Angela W. 1998. *Biting the hand that feeds? The social construction of adolescent violence toward parents as a social problem.* Master of Arts Thesis, Sociology, University of New Brunswick, Fredericton.

Gallagher, Eddie. 2004. "Parents victimised by their children." *Australia and New Zealand Journal of Family Therapy* 25, 1: 1–12. Available at <www.anzjft.com/ articles/discussions/gallagher-1.html>

*Globe and Mail.* 1999. Article on World Health Organization findings. Sept. 15.

Graham-Bermann, S.A. 1998. "The impact of woman abuse on children's social development: Research and theoretical perspectives." In George W. Holden, A. Geffner and Ernest N. Jouriles (eds.), *Children Exposed to Marital Violence: Theory, Research, and Applied Issues.* Washington, DC: American Psychological Association.

Hagan, John. 1991. "Destiny and drift: Subcultural preferences, status attainments, and the risks and rewards of youth." *American Sociological Review* 56: 567–582.

Hall, G. Stanley. 1904. *Adolescence.* New York: Appleton.

Harbin, H.T., and D. Madden. 1979. "Battered parents: A new syndrome." *American Journal of Psychiatry* 136: 1288–1291.

Health Canada. 1999. "Statistical Report on the Health of Canadians." Health Canada, Ottawa.

Heide, K.M.T. 1993. "Parents who get killed and the children who kill them." *Journal of Interpersonal Violence* 8: 531–544.

Hewlett, Sylvia Ann, and Cornell West. 1998. *The War Against Parents*. New York: Houghton Mifflin.

Hughes, H.M., D. Parkinson, and M. Vargo. 1989. "Witnessing spousal abuse and experiencing physical abuse: A 'double whammy'?" *Journal of Family Violence* 4: 197–209.

Jaffe, P.G., D. Wolfe, and S.K. Wilson. 1990. *Children of Battered Women*. Newbury Park, CA: Sage.

Kelly, Katherine, and Mark Totten. 2002. *When Children Kill: A Social-psychological Study of Youth Homicide*. Peterborough: Broadview Press.

Kerig, P.K. 1999. "Gender issues in the effects of exposure to violence on children." *Journal of Emotional Abuse* 1: 87–105.

Kerstetter, Steve. 2001. *BC home to greatest wealth gap in Canada*. Vancouver: Canadian Centre for Policy Alternatives.

Kratcoski, Peter C. 1984. "Perspectives on intrafamily violence." *Human Relations* 37: 443–454.

———. 1982. "Child Abuse and Violence Against the Family." *Child Welfare* LX1, 7: 435–443.

Kumagai, F. 1981. "Filial violence: A peculiar parent-child relationship in the Japanese family today." *Journal of Comparative Family Studies* 12: 337–349.

Lee, Marc. 2001. *Are we all capitalists now? The distribution of wealth in Canada*. Ottawa: Canadian Centre for Policy Alternatives.

Libon, M.D. 1989. "Adolescent-to-parent violence: An investigation of family environment, empathy and disengagement among adjudicated adolescents. *Dissertation Abstracts International* 49(7).

Livingston, L.R. 1986. "Children's violence to single mothers." *Journal of Sociology and Social Welfare* 13: 920–933.

Lotz, Roy, and Leona Lee. 1999. "Sociability, school experience, and delinquency." *Youth and Society* 31: 199–223.

Maker, A.H., M. Kemmelmeier, and C. Peterson. 1998. "Long-term psychological consequences in women of witnessing parental physical conflict and experiencing abuse in childhood." *Journal of Interpersonal Violence* 13: 574–589.

Mason, Paul, and Randi Kreger. 1998. *Stop Walking On Eggshells*. Oakland, CA: New Harbinger Publications.

Micucci, J.A. 1995. "Adolescents who assault their parents: A family systems approach to treatment." *Psychotherapy* 32: 154–161.

Monk, Peter. 1997. *Adolescent-To-Parent Violence: A Qualitative Analysis of Emerging Themes*. Thesis for Master of Social Work, University of British Columbia, Victoria.

Ney, P., and D. Mulvihill. 1982. "Case report on parent abuse." *Victimology* 7:

194–198.

Omer, Haim. 2000. *Parental Presence: Reclaiming a Leadership Role in Bringing Up Our Children*. Phoenix: Zeig, Tucker and Co.

Pagelow, M.D. 1989. "The incidence and prevalence of criminal abuse of other family members." In Lloyd Ohlin and Michael Tonry (eds.), *Family Violence*, vol. 2. Chicago: University of Chicago Press.

Patterson, G.R. 1980. "Mothers: The unacknowledged victims." *Monograph of the Society for Research in Child Development,* 45: 1–47.

_____. 1982. *A Social Learning Approach: Coercive Family Process*. Eugene, Oregon: Castalia.

Paulson, Morris J., Robert H. Coombs and John Landsverk. 1990. "Youth who physically assault their parents." *Journal of Family Violence* 5: 121–131.

Peek, Charles W., Judith L. Fischer and Jeannie S. Kidwell. 1985. "Teenage violence towards parents: A neglected dimension of family violence." *Journal of Marriage and the Family* 47: 1051–1058.

Pipher, Mary. 1994. *Reviving Ophelia: Saving the Selves of Adolescent Girls*. New York: Ballantine Books.

Pizzey, Erin. 1977. *Scream Quietly or the Neighbours Will Hear*. Short Hills, NJ: Enslow.

Pottie Bunge, V., and D. Locke. 2000. "Family Violence in Canada: A Statistical Profile, 2000." Statistics Canada, Ottawa.

Price, Jerome. 1996. *Power and Compassion: Working with Difficult Adolescents and Abused Parents*. New York: Guilford Press.

Price, Jerome, and Barbara Cottrell. 2002. *Power and Compassion: Helping Abused Parents Deal With Aggressive Teens*. Workshop. Maritime School of Social Work, Dalhousie University, Halifax, Nova Scotia. July.

Reuter, M.A., and R.D. Conger. 1995. "Interaction style: Problem-solving behavior, and family problem-solving effectiveness." *Child Development* 66: 98–115.

Rybski, Nancy Carole. 1998. *An evaluation of a family group therapy program for domestically violent adolescents*. Ph.D. Thesis, School of Family and Consumer Resources, University of Arizona.

Salts, C.J., B.W. Lindholm, H.W. Goddard, and S. Duncan. 1995. "Predictive variables of violent behaviour in adolescent males." *Youth and Society* 26: 377–399.

Sears, R., E. Macoby and H. Levin. 1957. *Patterns of Child Rearing*. Palo Alto, CA: Stanford University Press.

Shulman, Samuel, and Inge Seiffge-Krenke. 1997. *Fathers and Adolescents: Developmental and Clinical Perspectives*. London and New York: Routledge.

Simons, R.L., C. Wu, C. Johnson, and R.D. Conger. 1995. "A test of various perspectives on the intergenerational transmission of domestic violence." *Criminology* 33: 141–172.

Subrahmanyam, Kaveri, Robert E. Kraut, Patricia M. Greenfield, and Elisheva F. Gross. 2000. "The impact of home computer use on children's activities and development." *The Future of Children* 10: 123–144.

Sudermann, Marlies, and Peter Jaffe. 1999. *A Handbook for Health and Social Service Providers and Educators on Children Exposed to Woman Abuse/Family Violence.* Health Canada, Ottawa.

Taylor, Shelley E., Laura Cousino Klein, Brian P. Lewis, Tara L. Gruenewald, Regan A.R. Gurung, and John A. Updegraff. 2000. "Biobehavioral responses to stress in females: Tend-and-befriend, not fight-or-flight." *Psychological Review* 107, 3: 411–429.

Totten, Mark. 2003. *Youth and Violence.* Health Canada, Ottawa.

_____. 2000. *Guys, Gangs and Girlfriend Abuse.* Toronto: Broadview Press.

Walker, L.E. 1983. "The battered woman syndrome." In D. Finkelhor, R. Gelles, G.T. Hotaling, and M.A. Straus (eds.), *The Dark Side of Families: Current Family Violence Research.* Beverly Hills, CA: Sage.

Warren, C. 1978. "Parent batterers: Adolescent violence and the family." Anaheim, CA: *Pacific Sociological Association*

Wells, M.G. 1987. "Adolescent violence against parents: An assessment." *Family Therapy* 14: 125–133.

West, Cornel. 1993. *Race Matters.* Boston: Beacon Press.

# Index

Absent parents 41, 42, 46, 82, 84
Advertising 81, 90, 97
Advocacy 121
Age 20, 41, 50, 57, 73, 74
Agnew, R. 20, 40, 42, 45, 48, 72-74, 78
Aggression, levels of 10
    parents 22, 46, 48, 49, 75
    teens 18, 19, 50, 69, 70, 72, 73,75-78, 100, 114, 117, 122, 125, 135, 137, 139
Alibhai-Brown, Yasmin 1, 89
Allahar, A.L. 95
Ambert, Anne-Marie 57
Anxiety and despair 12, 14, 25, 45, 56, 57, 60, 61, 82, 88, 90, 92, 94, 99, 100, 105, 111, 113, 116, 119, 126, 128, 129, 132, 133, 140, 144, 151, 157, 158
Arrigo, M.J. 20
Artz, Sibylle 72, 75, 76
Attention Deficit Disorder (ADD), Attention Deficit Hyperactivity Disorder (ADHD) 27, 29, 35, 83, 99, 100
Authoritarian parenting 42, 44, 53, 84, 95
Authority 22, 41, 42, 82, 91, 96, 97, 101, 104, 127, 128, 144

Bandura, A. 74
Barber, Bonnie L. 40
Barkley, Jacqueline 89

Bass, Ellen 47
Blame/blaming 21, 49, 51, 54, 57, 58, 61, 76, 77, 88, 92, 98, 99, 101, 103-109, 117, 121, 122, 125-127, 129, 139, 151, 152, 157, 158
Boundaries and separation 18, 22, 25, 42, 46, 48, 49, 53, 97, 103-105, 120, 121, 128, 132, 135, 143
Boy children 2, 13, 41, 72, 74, 78, 82, 93, 123
Brezina, T. 44, 77, 78
Browne, K.D. 77, 78
Bullying 12, 80, 82, 150
Bushwall, P. 52, 78, 94

Caplan, P.J. 57
Carlsmith, J. 52, 78, 94
Carlson, B.E. 50, 78
Cazenave, N.A 40
Charles, A.V. 40, 42, 45, 72, 73, 78, 95
Child protection agencies 106, 113-116, 120, 122, 138
Collusion 123, 139
Compassion 88, 97, 101, 110, 128, 129, 141, 155, 157, 159
Conduct disorders 42, 83, 100, 110
Conger, R.D. 50
Consequences 41, 42, 44, 46, 53, 55, 70, 96, 97, 110, 112, 123, 125, 132, 133, 135, 138, 140, 143, 145
Coombs, Robert H. 20, 40, 45, 48, 73, 74, 79

Cornell, C.P. 20, 40, 44, 45, 72, 74, 78

Côté, J.E. 95

Cottrell, Barbara 2, 3, 10, 13, 16, 20, 24, 126

Counselling and therapy 10, 39, 100, 107-109, 116, 118, 120-129, 132, 139, 146, 152

Coupland, Douglas 92, 95

Criminal justice system 19, 109, 111, 112

Culture and class 21, 69, 88, 90

Culture, popular 15, 89-91

Culture and race 21, 40, 57, 69, 141

Culture of violence 93

Dauvergne, Mia 75, 77

Davis, Laura 47

Definition of parent abuse 16, 17

Dekeseredy, Walter S. 19

Denial 22, 61, 103, 139, 160, 161

Duncan, S. 45

Disabilities and disorders,
    learning 38, 83
    physical 17

Divorce and separation 25, 54, 94, 116, 125

Dornbusch, S. 52, 78, 94

Eccles, Jacqueline S. 40

Eckstein, Nancy J. 22, 40, 45, 74, 79

Edleson, J.L. 75

Enang, Josephine 40, 44

Entitlement 41, 43, 51, 58

Evans, E.D 45, 72, 78

Exposure to violence 50, 51, 53, 71, 75, 77, 93, 129

Fathers and stepfathers 45-56, 74, 75, 77, 125

Fear, for children 47, 49, 55, 97, 113, 129, 133
    of children 11, 12, 17, 20, 32, 49, 55, 59, 116, 129

of losing children 37, 113

Financial abuse 15, 17, 50

Fischer, Judith L. 20, 41, 44, 45, 74, 78

Frizzell, Angela W. 17

Gallagher, Eddie 40, 41, 43, 45, 50, 51, 72, 81, 109, 121, 123, 124

Gelles, R.J. 20, 40, 44, 45, 72, 74, 78

Girl children 41. 72-76, 78, 81

Goddard, H.W. 45

Graham-Bermann, S.A. 75

Greenfield, Patricia M. 93

Gross, Elisheva F. 93

Gross, R. 52, 78, 94

Gruenewald, Tara L. 49

Guidance counsellors 131, 136

Gurung, Regan A.R. 49

Guilt 1, 43, 48, 50, 51, 57, 61, 78, 83, 84, 90, 99, 103, 104, 109, 116, 128, 129, 132, 134, 138, 145, 151

Hagan, John 40

Hall, G. Stanley 18

Hamilton, C.E. 77, 78

Harbin, H.T. 19, 41, 42, 45, 48, 72-74, 84

Hastorf, A. 52, 78, 94

Heide, K.M.T. 16

Hewlett, Sylvia Ann 80, 91, 93, 94

Homophobia 108, 113

Hope 25, 30, 62, 126, 133

Hughes, H.M. 75

Huguley, S. 20, 40, 42, 45, 48, 72-74, 78

Immigrant parents 40, 44, 61, 113, 169

Isolation 1, 99, 117, 133, 134, 143, 149, 159

Jaffe, Peter 50, 75, 77

Johnson, C. 50

Johnson, Holly 92, 95

Kelly, Katherine 16
Kemmelmeier, M. 75
Kerig, P.K. 75
Kerstetter, Steve. 94
Kidwell, Jeannie S. 20, 41, 44, 45,
    74, 78
Klein, Laura Cousino 49
Kratcoski, Peter C. 44, 45, 78
Kraut, Robert E. 93
Kreger, Randi 130
Kumagai, F. 41, 45, 48, 73

Labelling 79, 99, 100, 107, 122
Landsverk, John 20, 40, 45, 48, 73,
    74, 79
Lay counsellors 118
Leadership, community 91, 120, 136
    parental 1, 21, 22, 42, 57, 80, 88,
    96-98, 157, 159
Lee, Leona 40
Lee, Marc 94
Leiderman, H. 52, 78, 94
Lesbians 108
Levin, H. 19
Lewis, Brian P. 49
Libon, M.D. 78
Lindholm, B.W. 45
Livingston, L.R. 41, 45, 78
Locke, D. 50
Lotz, Roy 40

Macoby, E. 19
Madden, D. 19, 41, 42, 45, 48, 72-
    74, 84
Maker, A.H. 75
Manipulation 6, 12, 13, 14, 56, 99,
    109, 125
Marital conflict 52, 53, 55, 124, 170
Mason, Paul 130
Media 21, 77, 89, 91-93, 95, 125,
    153
Mediation and restorative justice

119, 120
Medication 13, 27, 29, 60, 100, 101,
    130
Meditation 132
Mental health/disabilities 22, 58, 60,
    71, 72, 78, 83-85, 99, 101, 107,
    130, 144, 158
Mental health services 19, 99, 100,
    106-108, 116, 120, 121, 124, 127,
    130, 148
Micucci, J.A. 42
Monk, Peter 3, 17, 23, 112, 139,
    140, 141
Mulvihill, D. 42
Murray, A. 40

Ney, P. 42

Omer, Haim 3, 13, 40, 42, 52, 55,
    58, 97, 107, 129, 136, 138

Pagelow, M.D. 20, 45
Parental absence 41, 42, 46, 82, 84
Parenting Classes 121
Parkinson, D. 75
Patterson, G.R. 46, 78
Paulson, Morris J. 20, 40, 45, 48, 73,
    74, 79
Peek, Charles W. 20, 41, 44, 45, 74,
    78
Peer pressure 71, 79, 80-82, 84, 139
Peers 22, 40, 42, 47, 54, 71, 78-82,
    84, 97, 125, 136, 139
Peterson, C. 75
Permissive parenting 41-44, 53, 61,
    84, 97, 158
Pets 55
Physical abuse 10-13, 17, 19, 20, 23,
    40, 43-44, 47-51, 59, 63, 72-74,
    76-78, 81, 84, 110-112, 139, 141
Pipher, Mary 42, 77, 83
Pizzey, Erin 21
Plaus, Xavier 73, 77, 78, 80
Police 18-21, 43, 90, 109-116, 133,

138
Pottie Bunge, V. 50
Poverty 40, 93, 94, 127
Price, Jerome 10, 13, 22, 41, 52, 54,
  95, 96, 99-101, 118, 122-124,
  126-129, 137, 163
Psychological/emotional abuse 10-
  14, 16, 17, 39, 51, 77, 78

Racism 113, 127, 158
Remorse 14, 82-84, 140
Removing teens from home 49, 50,
  113, 113-115, 144, 145
Resisting authority 18, 90, 123, 138
Resources 21, 57, 91, 93, 94, 97,
  106, 120, 122, 125, 147, 160
Reuter, M.A. 50
Ritter, P. 52, 78, 94
Rybski, Nancy Carole 124

Salts, C.J. 45
Scapegoating 98
Schools 5, 16, 22, 40, 59, 66, 78-80,
  82, 84, 98-100, 116, 117, 136-
  138, 148
Sears, R. 19
Seiffge-Krenke, Inge 55, 75
Self-care, teens 13, 43
  parents 48, 127, 132, 155
Self-destructive behaviour 13, 42,
  136
Self-esteem, teens 42, 77, 126
Sexual abuse 16, 50, 77, 78
Shulman, Samuel 55, 75
Siblings 55, 56, 70, 77, 84, 113, 115,
  118, 145
Simons, R.L. 50
Single parents 45, 48, 61, 94, 113,

116, 145
Social workers 6, 23, 37, 39, 43, 89,
  97, 115, 121, 141, 142
Step-parents 45, 52, 77
Straus, M.A. 40
Subrahmanyam, Kaveri 93
Substance use/abuse 13, 56, 57, 60,
  78, 79, 82-85, 94, 116, 126, 133
Sudermann, Marlies 75, 77
Suicide threats 11, 15, 136
Support groups 119, 156, 159

Taylor, Shelley E. 49
Theories 124, 125
Threats of consequences 110, 112,
  138, 141
  of not being a good mother 57,
  104
  from teens 10-14, 22, 23, 40, 43,
  53, 70, 75, 79, 81, 82, 95, 137,
  138
Totten, Mark 16, 76, 77, 82, 89

Updegraff, John A. 49

Vargo, M. 75
Verbal abuse 2, 12, 17, 18, 43, 48,
  51, 56, 58

Walker, L.E. 84
Warren, C. 74
Warren-Sohlberg, L. 45, 72, 78
Wells, M.G. 45, 77, 78
West, Cornell 80, 91-94
Wilson, S.K. 50, 75
Wolfe, D. 75
Wu, C. 50

# Nuthouse Episode